PRAISE FOR PATRICK O'NEIL

"*Gun, Needle, Spoon* is a wild, tender ride of a memoir that you'll never forget. Fierce, funny, and true to the bone, O'Neil's voice is as real and memorable as they come. Read it."

—Emily Rapp, author of *The Still Point of the Turning World*

"*Gun, Needle, Spoon* is like having a near-death experience...with Patrick O'Neil's life flashing before your eyes."

—Craig Clevenger, author of *The Contortionist's Handbook* and *Dermaphoria*

"*Gun, Needle, Spoon* grabs the reader from the very start and doesn't let up until you've turned the last page and are left moved, disturbed, and a little out of breath. This harrowing, brutally honest, and unexpectedly redemptive debut firmly establishes O'Neil as a truly original voice in contemporary literature."

—Rob Roberge, author of *The Cost of Living*

"Reads like a novel, a crazy, funny, perverse, heartbreaking memoir you're both relieved and reluctant to have finished. The jarring truth that it all actually happened is what takes it one step beyond into the realm of the mythic. You must read this."

—Scott Phillips, author of *Hop Alley* and *Cottonwood*

"*Gun, Needle, Spoon* is told the only way drug memoir should be told: nonlinear and disjointed. Paranoia is your friend. A gun is your ATM card. And like every drug story, it's a love story, told through a hole in the arm."

—Bucky Sinister, author of *King of the Roadkills* and *Get Up*

"Patrick O'Neil has managed the unusual feat of writing about a battle-scarred life with both toughness and vulnerability, but without posturing or sentimentality. *Gun, Needle, Spoon* brings to mind Denis Johnson and Jim Carroll without sounding exactly like either. This book has the spare, lean energy of classic crime writing and is both entertaining and full of insight. A great read."

—Jesse Michaels, Operation Ivy

GUN
NEEDLE
SPOON

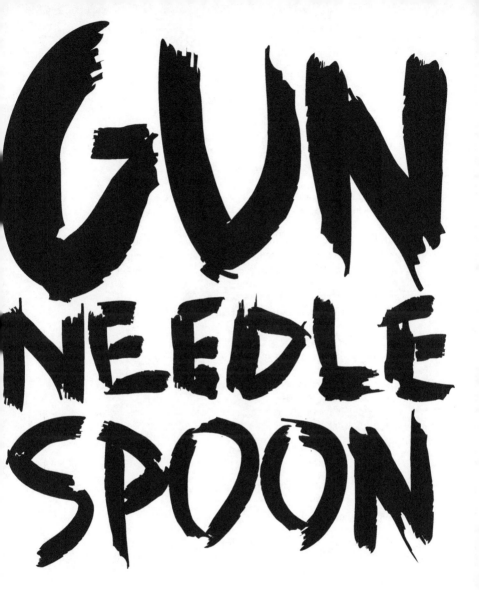

GUN
NEEDLE
SPOON

a memoir

PATRICK O'NEIL

DZANC
BOOKS

DZANC BOOKS

5220 Dexter Ann Arbor Rd.
Ann Arbor, MI 48103
www.dzancbooks.org

Library of Congress Cataloging-in-Publication Data

O'Neil, Patrick, 1956-
  Gun, needle, spoon : (a memoir) / by Patrick O'Neil.
    page cm
  1. O'Neil, Patrick, 1956- 2. Drug addicts--Biography. 3. Heroin. 4. Drug addiction. I. Title.
  HV5822.I14O54 2015
  362.29'3092--dc23
  [B]

                                    2014013384

Published 2015 by Dzanc Books
ISBN: 978-1936873575
First U.S. edition: June 2015

Printed in the United States of America

10   9   8   7   6   5   4   3   2   1

Portions and/or excerpts of the memoir were previously published in the following publications: The chapter "Last Day" was published in *New Plains Review*, Fall Issue, 2010. The chapter "Learning New Behaviors" was published as "Las Vegas, 1966" in *The Survivor Chronicles*, May Issue, 2010. The chapter "Wake Up" was published in *The Coachella Review*, Fall Issue, 2010. And the chapter "Looking Back: Anxiety's Greatest Hits" was published in *Sensitive Skin*, Number 10, 2013, and as "The Scent of Death" in *The Citron Review*, September Issue, 2009.

For Jenn

PART ONE

"I never thought I was gonna live to thirty."

—*Patti Smith*

Last Day

Chunks of the door frame fly through the air and fall on either side of me. I stand there, immobile. A hundred cops outside, some in uniform, some not, guns drawn, faces and bodies tense. A tall, heavyset blond police officer steps forward through the doorway and smacks me in the face with the butt of her shotgun as more cops push past her and into the apartment. I lie on the floor, a foot across my throat, a knee in my groin, a shotgun and a 9mm leveled at my head.

A plainclothes policeman shouts, "Where are the guns, motherfucker!" His badge, hanging loosely on a chain around his neck, swings back and forth over my face. "Are you alone?" asks another. Before I can reply I hear Jenny, oblivious, slurring her words, wondering what all the noise is about. A finger to his lips, the plainclothes cop points toward the bedroom. My stomach tightens and I fear what the cops will do to Jenny if I don't try and make her understand what is happening. I put up my hand, palm out, motioning for him to stop.

"Jenny? Jenny!" I shout. "Could you come out here?"

"What for?" she asks, and then there's the crash of breaking glass, furniture being shoved, voices shouting for her to get down on the floor. They must be coming in through the windows. Then someone's turning me over, handcuffing my arms behind my back, and I'm being lifted—half carried, half dragged—out into daylight.

On the street in front of my apartment building are a dozen police cars, lights flashing, radios blaring. A small group of my neighbors watches from down the block, a few pointing at me as I'm dragged to the nearest patrol car. Over my shoulder I can see my friend Dolan spread-eagled, being searched on the hood of another car.

Tossed into the back seat, I try to sit up and ask the nearest cop for a cigarette. He slams the door in my face. A minute later a man in a suit walks up, opens the door, introduces himself as a detective and apologizes for the other cop's behavior. Then he calls me by my name, says he's been watching me for some time now. "I'll see you down at the station later on tonight, Mister O'Neil," he says, then he shuts the door, tells the driver to take me downtown, and stands there staring at me through the window as we drive away.

I keep thinking that this isn't real. That none of this is happening. That the cop who's driving the car will pull over to the curb, unlock the handcuffs, and set me free. Every turn of the wheel makes me lose my balance and I push up and off the seat with my elbows to keep myself upright. The cuffs dig into my skin. The monotone of the police dispatcher's voice coming out of the radio is the only sound piercing the oppressive atmosphere in the car. My heart pounds, the motor accelerates, an abrupt stop sends me crashing into the metal cage that separates the back from the front.

I feel helpless. I feel like screaming. I feel like crying, only I don't know how. I want a cigarette so bad I can't think of anything else. I start to get angry. I start yelling. I call the cop a motherfucker, tell him that this is all a mistake, that I haven't done anything. I kick the cage, tell him he's got to believe me.

San Francisco passes by: the Ferry Building, the waterfront, the Bay Bridge, Harrison Street. We arrive at a parking lot behind the Hall of Justice, pull into a space marked Official Vehicles Only. The cop opens my door and I feel the cool air against my naked chest. Without saying a word, he grabs my arm and drags me out onto the ground. Two more cops walk up and there's a kick to the ribs, sharp pain in my shoulders as I'm raised up off the ground to my feet and shoved toward a large metal door.

One cop pushes the intercom button and waves at the camera above our heads. The other presses my face against the coarse stucco wall, his gloved hand firmly on the back of my head. With a mechanized hiss, the sally port slides open and the smell of jail hits me: dirty feet, unwashed bodies, rancid food, exhaust fumes, and human shit. Pushed along by a hand on my shoulder, I stumble down a hall lined with empty holding cells. The cop signs a couple of forms at the booking desk before handing me off to the sheriffs who run the jail. My anxiety had been holding the heroin in check, but now the pills I also took are starting to kick in and I'm fading. Slurring, I mumble my name, address, social security number as a woman in uniform types it all into a computer.

Herded through a maze of desks and filing cabinets, I lose my bearings. An older deputy, bald with glasses, tells me it's almost over and I wonder just what he means. One of the sheriffs grabs hold of my fingers as if they weren't attached to me and shoves them in black ink, pressing the tips to a sheet of paper and leaving smudged imprints on the appropriate squares. Someone hands me a brown paper towel and I try to wipe the blackness from my fingertips. My surroundings are becoming more and more unfocused, the meaning of what is going on increasingly vague. A deputy gives me a shirt with frayed cuffs. I open my eyes and a flashbulb erupts, temporarily blinding me. I'm turned to my left: profile shot. Metal hitting metal, the sound of a door closing. The constant roar of the jail decreases to a low growl. Half crouched, my back against the wall, I feel a hard surface and collapse.

Exhausted, I nod off into a dream about a large Siamese cat that rubs against my body, her fur soft on my skin. She tells me she's been starved for days and stands on my chest screaming for me to feed her. Our protruding rib cages mesh together, her paws embed themselves in my skin. I'm confused as to why she doesn't just run away when she has the chance. I reach to pet her and feel my own cold skin taut against my bones. Running my fingers along my ribs, I press the bottom of my sternum and hear it click. I try to light a cigarette with the cat's face. Its claws tear at my arms and they start to bleed.

With a jolt I wake up freezing on a cement slab that sticks out of the wall, forming a bench. I look for the cat, but she's gone. Drool runs down the side of my face, and my mouth tastes metallic, bad as the air I'm breathing. It takes a minute for me to realize where I am. I want a cigarette really bad, and I want to go back to sleep. I want to be anywhere but on this bench in this fucking holding cell. Sitting up, I rub my eyes and look out through the wire-mesh-reinforced windows. I can see Dolan in a cell across the hall. He flashes me a weak smile. I can tell from his eyes that he's as worried as I am. Twelve years younger than me, he's less experienced. But that hasn't kept him from driving the getaway car for most of my recent holdups. Sitting upright makes my head hurt. I want a cigarette. I think about Jenny, wonder where she is, if she's okay. Last time I saw her she was in handcuffs being led to a cop car. I could see her head moving. Probably giving the cop an earful of shit.

Thinking of her makes me miss home, a ground-floor garden apartment in the back of a three-story building in the Marina District—a once nondescript upper-middle-class neighborhood that reinvented itself as a yuppie stronghold after the '89 earthquake. Not the most typical of locations to find an apartment full of dope fiends, and maybe that's why we'd been able to go unnoticed for so long. Nobody expects us to be living there, especially not the landlord, who's been lied to so many times about the rent that he's practically given up ever seeing it.

I've been living there for about two years. Me and my girlfriend, Jenny. Twenty-one years old and just as strung out on heroin as I am, beautiful in a pasty-face, walking-dead junkie-chic sort of way. I'd met her three years earlier coming off a horrendous speed run I'd started so I could get away with shooting less heroin. I hadn't slept in months when she asked me if I could get her some dope.

A succession of nodded-out friends like Dolan had been living with us, using the walk-in closet as a place to crash. These days, though, no one could stand staying with us. Even other drug addicts couldn't deal with our insanity, our demands for money. We smoked all their cigarettes and used up whatever else they might have. All day we'd lie together side by side in the bedroom on the futon. Jenny, in a nod, continually burned herself or the bed with lit cigarettes—small fires and red welts becoming daily occurrences. Over on my side I'd ignore her until I felt flames, and then I'd roll over and put out whatever was on fire.

Jesus, Jenny, I wonder where you are. She's never been to jail, never dealt with cops. I can only imagine the bullshit they're putting her through.

The cell door opens. "O'Neil!" yells a gruff-looking deputy with a clipboard in his hand, and I look up.

"Where am I going?" I ask. It doesn't really matter, and the look on the deputy's face tells me he doesn't care either. We walk down the corridor to an unmarked elevator. "Against the wall," he commands. I turn, face the wall, raise my arms. Taking my right hand, he circles the handcuff around my wrist, pulls the other down, cuffs it too. The elevator door opens. It's dirty inside and smells like piss. The deputy motions for me to enter, and when I hesitate he pushes me in against the back wall. I hear the door close, feel the elevator car start to rise.

"You a tough guy?" taunts the deputy. I stare at the wall, say nothing. There's no point getting into it with this guy. I'm handcuffed, he's not; I'm under arrest, he's an officer of the law. And I'm not a tough guy, never said I was. The elevator shudders to a stop and he pulls me out into a corridor. Hand clamped around the back of my neck, he leads me through a door with Robbery Detail written across it in black letters with gold trim. Inside there are four or five empty desks. A man at a computer, his shirtsleeves rolled up to the elbows, looks over at us as he continues to type. "Put him there," he says, pointing to a chair by a desk in the middle of the room.

I'm suddenly very tired. I can feel that familiar emptiness creeping in. It's not that the drugs have worn off yet. More like my anxiety has kicked in full force. I can't count the number of nights when I'd be asleep at home and then suddenly, so gripped with fear of this exact moment I'd all of a sudden be awake, sitting up all in one motion, holding my chest as my heart fought to burst through my rib cage. Somewhere deep down, whether I wanted to admit it or not, I knew all this was coming. I knew someday I'd be sitting here in handcuffs.

There was a time when I tried selling drugs to support Jenny's and my habits, but we'd always end up doing all the drugs before

I could sell them. Now and then I'd get a temporary gig working construction or painting houses, but I'd constantly screw it up. Dope sick and unable to make it to work on time, I'd get fired or stop showing up. Strung out as I was, I couldn't hold down a regular job. Besides, your average nine-to-five doesn't pay anywhere near the hundreds of dollars a day it takes to afford an extensive heroin habit, much less two.

One rainy day, jonesing for a fix, out of options and out of my mind, me and a friend walked into a movie theater with a gun someone had traded me for dope and we robbed the ticket booth and the concession stand. When we got home I discovered we'd netted six hundred dollars. It had taken us twenty minutes at the most to drive there, pull the job, and drive back. After that it was even easier. We pulled off a couple of liquor stores and a 7-11. Then, during a gas station holdup, the attendant grabbed a gun from under the counter and almost shot me. Made me think that before I got killed for a few hundred dollars I'd better set my sights higher, go where the real money was.

A week later I was at a bank cashing a check from a day's worth of grueling manual labor I vowed I'd never do again, and I was watching the teller as she counted out my money from a stack of twenties in her hand. When she gave it to me I took my time recounting while making a mental note of which drawer she returned the stack of twenties to. Our transaction completed, I stood off to the side and scoped out the lack of a security guard and where each of the cameras were. When I walked outside I realized the bank's location on a busy street corner with tons of traffic made it perfect for me to slip into the crowd for an easy getaway. The next day I pulled my first bank job, netting a few thousand dollars in ninety seconds.

After a couple more I realized I was dressed exactly the same as in daily life and it wouldn't be hard for the cops to spot me. So I got creative and started going in disguise: fake beard and baseball cap with a phony ponytail out the back; dressed in a uniform as a security guard; posing as a businessman, complete with three-piece suit and an attaché case. Drop a note in front of the teller, mention the gun, and walk right out the front door into a waiting car. Those days I had more people around me, dope fiends I thought I could count on to watch my back for a portion of the take.

Bank jobs take planning and a somewhat alert state of mind. And back then I wasn't so scattered. I was able to bide my time, hang around outside, watch and take notes on what time the guards took their breaks, what time the armored trucks came by and delivered the money. What times the banks were crowded, when the managers were gone. I parked the car across the street, pulled out a newspaper, pad of paper, and a pencil; I'd smoke cigarettes, shoot some dope if no one was watching.

After a while I started running out of banks to hit. Then one day, sitting in front of a bank I'd robbed twice before, I noticed shopkeepers taking bank bags up to the merchant's window, depositing the day's take from their stores. I started following them from the bank to their businesses. Did the same sort of surveillance I'd done at the banks and slowly figured out their routines, saw when their stores did the most business. I always had two or three alternative locations to rob. If one wasn't ready, another would be. I kept myself busy, working different neighborhoods with a driver, in and out quickly. Making it hard to be caught.

But then I started slacking off. Everyone was scared, dead, or in jail, and I was on my own. I began seeing every cash register out there as an ATM—except instead of a debit card, I used a gun. Now, every day first thing, I'd go out and hold up a liquor or grocery store, and that money would keep us in drugs and cigarettes for the next twenty-four hours. Every once in a while Dolan would show up needing cash and offering to drive, and we'd pull off a heist.

Dolan was the last person who'd still do crimes with me. I was so out of it that anyone else would be too nervous to even drive, let alone sit next to me with my loaded gun. Jenny couldn't drive—she could barely leave the apartment—or she would've gone with me. Instead she sat waiting for me to get home, waiting for the dope man to deliver, waiting while I cooked the dope, her arm stretched out, waiting for the needle to pierce her skin, waiting for that high.

There's a tap on my shoulder. "O'Neil," says the detective from in front of my house. "Feel like talking?" he asks.

"Could use a cigarette," I tell him.

"Can't smoke in here. Not allowed in any State of California building."

"Yeah, I'd hate to break the law," I say. That makes him laugh. He takes his jacket off and sits down across the desk from me.

"You know why you're here, right?"

"Got a pretty good idea," I say and immediately regret admitting even that much.

"You're in a lot of trouble. When this is over you'll be looking at doing some time in prison. I can help, if you let me."

I stare at him. He stares back. We sit there in silence. My stomach hurts, my eyes start to water, I sneeze. I'm going into the first stages of withdrawal from heroin. With my habit I have to shoot up every four hours. Valium and Klonopin help, keep me loaded longer, but in the end it's heroin I'm addicted to. That's what my body craves.

"Want to make a statement? Get it over with, tell me about it? I'm going to know the whole story anyway."

"I could still use that cigarette."

With a shrug he reaches for the phone on his desk, looks at me, pushes in a number, waits. "Tell the Feds we're ready," he says, then hangs up and looks at me, stares into my eyes. "Feds might want to pick up your case, prosecute the bank robberies instead of us. You're getting dope sick, aren't you?"

There was a time I'd claim to be a bank robber. This sure as hell wasn't one of them. I looked down at my feet to avoid any more eye contact. In the back of my mind I kept replaying the last robbery. Kept thinking how I'd fucked it up. How I should've done things differently.

It'd taken me forever to get out of the house. I'd shot dope, smoked coke, taken some Valiums and then a hit of speed in the hopes that would give me the energy I needed. Dolan was pacing, nervously waiting for me. I checked my gun and threw on a suit.

"Let's fuckin' do this," I said.

Outside of the movie theater I pulled a ski mask over my head and stepped out of the car. The Presidio was one of those arthouse theaters that showed foreign films and served espressos and real buttered popcorn. It was one of several I kept my eye on as a potential hit. Most weekends they'd wait until Monday to deposit everything at once. I knew this because I'd watched them from a café across the street. Two weekends running they'd stuck to the same pattern: the owner walking the weekend deposit next door to the bank.

I shoved open the door with my shoulder and stormed into the lobby shouting that this was a holdup, brandishing the gun. A young woman at the ticket counter started at me. Another girl working the concession stand screamed.

"Where's the manager?"

"She just left," said the ticket girl.

I took what was in the till, less than four hundred dollars, and ran back outside. My getaway car was parked at the curb, wedged in between two other cars. I jumped in, yelling at Dolan for parking like an idiot. He slowly backed up and turned the wheel just as a city bus lumbered to a stop, blocking us in as it dislodged passengers. Pulling the ski mask off my face I turned to the sound of a woman screaming. The girl from the ticket counter was out in front of the theater pointing at me. For a few seconds we stared at each other. Then the bus moved, Dolan hit the gas, and I closed my eyes.

Out in the hall there's the sound of heels striking the floor. Two people walk into the room: a tall woman with a severe haircut and an amazing figure, and a man with gray hair and a thin mustache carrying a briefcase. Both of them wear dark suits, perfectly groomed. Emulating an air of superiority, they stride over to the desk; the man looks at the detective, the woman looks at me, then they look at each other.

"This O'Neil?" asks the man in disbelief.

"Yep, that's your bank robber."

The woman asks, "You a bank robber?" Her quizzical expression fades to concern. "You don't look like a bank robber. In fact, you don't look like you could rob anything."

I'd like to tell her thanks for the vote of confidence. That, yeah, she's right, I'm nothing but a loser. But even as stressed as I am, I can tell it's a ploy. She wants me to bite, take the bait, get angry, prove my criminal credibility by talking about all the jobs I've done. I don't say anything. I don't even ask her for a cigarette. These two mean business and I've watched enough movies and television shows to know that you don't offer information. Besides, I really don't care what they think of me.

The man pulls a thick binder out of his briefcase. "Got some photos we want you to look at," he says, handing the binder toward me. Jerking my head, I point with my eyes at my shoulder, trying to convey that my wrists are still handcuffed behind my back.

"Can we get the cuffs off this guy? He ain't going nowhere."

The detective looks at me, raises his eyebrows, puts a hand in his pocket. "I haven't got a key on me. Be right back." He gets up, walks out of the room.

The woman scans the pages in her hand. "You ever been to prison?"

"No one's even read me my Miranda rights," I say, and then wonder if I should have mentioned that fact.

The gray-haired FBI agent spreads open the binder on the desk in front of me and starts slowly turning the pages. "Here, look at these while we wait for the key."

Each page is a grainy blown-up surveillance photo. Most of them are black and white, some out of focus, some amazingly sharp. "Recognize anyone?" he asks.

After about fifteen pages, I see myself. Or, rather, I see a fuzzy picture from some odd overhead angle of me in a suit and tie, wearing sunglasses and a string mustache, my hair combed back. I'm carrying a gym bag. I look short, distorted; although the top of my head's in focus, I can't see my feet. I'm fascinated and I can't look away. I wonder how many more pictures of me he's got. The next one shows a giant black man carrying an AK-47 wearing a rainbow afro wig, a huge grin across his face. I laugh.

He stops turning the pages, looks at me. "You find this funny?"

"Ah, no," I say, "there's nothing funny about any of this." And, actually, I mean that.

"I don't think he's our man," says the woman. Her face is expressionless as she hands him the papers she's got in her hands. "I think we'd better re-evaluate this."

"Here you go," says the detective, who comes back into the room holding a set of keys. Looking up from packing the binder back into his case, the gray-haired agent shakes his head. "We're not going to be needing those." He looks over at the woman, who pulls the detective to the doorway and whispers in his ear. They both look over at me.

Then, shaking hands, the woman agent leaves with a nod, the gray-haired man follows her out. The detective walks to his desk and lifts the phone. "He's ready. Come get him." He sits, rubs his eyes. He pulls at his tie, drinks from a Styrofoam cup. "Looks like the State of California's got you."

I'm not sure what that means, and it doesn't really matter. My stomach is getting tight and there's that familiar taste in my throat that comes right before I get dope sick. Right before I start throwing up. Right before the diarrhea, the muscle spasms, the headaches, the cold sweats. At this moment I can't comprehend that the State of California's got anything in store for me as bad as what I'm about to go through.

The same angry-looking deputy arrives, motions me out the door, pushes me down the hall and into the elevator. Instead of going down to where we came from, we go up.

"Sixth floor, classification," he says to me, answering my unasked question. "They got a room with a view waiting for you."

I feel like throwing up, but I hold it in.

LEARNING NEW BEHAVIORS

The sun bleaches out everything. Takes all the colors and mutes them into echoes of their former selves, and beats relentlessly upon whoever dares venture outside. It is the desert after all—nothing but dirt and scruffy dried plants for miles. Yet there's a stuccoed steel and glass city built right in the middle, like somebody's idea of a joke. Hotels, nightclubs, and casinos erupting out of the desert, their marquees and glitzy neon façades making it hard to imagine this was once an endless expanse of nothing.

But before those fancy hotels and casinos, there's miles of gas stations and burger joints, auto repair shops and liquor stores. And then, off to the side of a dead-end street, next to an aging trailer park, there's a one-story adobe motel done up in a burnt sienna trim, its rooms stretched out in a long thin row. A dull green air-conditioning unit sticking out the bottom of each window trickles rust-colored water as if each of them was slowly bleeding to death on the sidewalk.

The motel's faded white doors and matching curtains hide whatever's going on inside. Buicks, Oldsmobiles, Chevys, and Fords sit out front, their heavy chrome bumpers reflecting glare into your eyes as inside the temperature rises ten or more degrees. The imitation leather seats absorbing the heat, and the orange

Union 76 balls on outstretched antennas seem frozen in time, not even the suggestion of a breeze out here.

Moving from the shade, you squint against the bright scorching sun. A glint of metal catches your eye. Across the flat expanse of shimmering black asphalt, a brand-new galvanized chain-link fence surrounds the smooth cement border of a kidney-shaped swimming pool—its glistening turquoise water an unspoken invitation of relief from the sun's heat.

A shiny black inner tube floating in the deep end frames the pasty, white-skinned boy lying on top with his head back, staring at the sky as his limbs dangle in the water, lying there half-conscious from the heat as the inner tube spins him around in a slow circle. A dab of freckles, a shock of red hair, his frail shoulders turning pink in the noonday sun. He turns to peel his back off the inner tube and this casual movement jackknifes his bony legs and arms together, sending his body through the center with a splash. A hand rises up out of the water attempting to grab hold of something solid—but finding only air, it quickly disappears.

He plunges into the cold blue void. The motel on the edge of the desert becomes a flat swirl on the surface of the water above. He drifts slowly through the yielding liquid. Air bubbles rise as the last gasp of air rushes out and catapults upward to join the abundance of oxygen on the surface. The engulfing turquoise fades to dark blue, purple, then black.

A slight pressure on my shoulder, then a quick sensation of rising. Suddenly the heat attacks the cold, numbing ache. Gasping for air, clear chlorinated water bubbles over my blue lips. Coughing as a hand pushes up against my stomach and rib cage in order to force the water out.

There's a rush of noise in my ears. A machine-like hum interspersed with the sound of people talking.

"Oh my god, is he okay?" asks my mother, a sense of annoyed urgency in her voice.

"He's fine," says my father. Another push on my stomach, more water pours out of me. I feel the sun on my face and somewhere there's the sound of a car starting.

"How long was he under?"

"I don't know," says my father. "But he's all right."

"You sure he's okay?"

"Don't worry, them who are meant to hang won't drown."

"What did you say?"

"I said he'll be all right."

A plane lazily glides across the sky. I feel hungry and think about a cheeseburger with pickles and that Thousand Island dressing all the burger places are now serving along with lettuce and a slice of tomato if you really want to get fancy. The towel wrapped around my shoulders feels coarse against my skin. The textured cement rough on the back of my thighs. All I can smell is chlorine, and my eyes burn. I look down, my legs dangling in the pool, and I think about being underwater and how comfortable almost dying felt.

"Can we go eat?" I ask. But no one's there to answer me.

What about the Farewell Drugs?

San Francisco, July 25, 1979

I light a cigarette and shift my eyes to Lee. "Fuck, last one," I say, and toss the crumpled pack in the gutter. It's four in the afternoon and we're walking on Market Street, heading to another movie theater.

"Fuckin' hungry," says Lee.

But then, Lee's always fucking hungry. It's like he's got animal instincts for three things: drugs, food, and sex—and not necessarily in that order. We've been hanging out, doing nothing since graduating art school. No jobs, no money, bumming cigarettes, scrounging off girlfriends, stealing rides on buses, and sneaking into movie theaters where friends work so we can waste another afternoon watching a triple feature of slasher and B-grade wannabe porn.

"Gimme a drag." Lee reaches for the cigarette. Seeing as it's the only one we got, I give it to him.

I'm twenty-one years old and fresh out of art school with a diploma in my hand, but I have no idea what the hell I want to do. Being an artist wasn't what I thought it was going to be, and really, I just don't know. Selling my art and myself and showing at galleries makes me feel like a fucking whore making gold yo-yos for the rich. None of the courses I took taught me anything so useful as how to survive as an artist.

"Gonna call Chris," says Lee. "Get us on the list for tonight."

"Who's playin'?"

"Does it matter?"

Lee's a photographer, a good photographer. We went to school together. A pretty boy: dark-complected, skinny, and tall. Lee gets all the women, and I stumble awkwardly in his wake. Eight years later he's going to be diagnosed with a brain tumor. One of those big ones they always compare to citrus fruits or baseballs, and after the operation he'll have this gigantic question mark of a scar etched into the back of his head and down his neck. In his late fifties, his health rapidly declining, he'll be a resident in an assisted-living center in Santa Monica. Endlessly staring at the TV, wasted on Oxycodones, avoiding my phone calls, and contemplating suicide.

But this is years before that. Lee is shooting publicity stills and live performances for a lot of rock and roll bands and has connections to get us into clubs, like Wolfgang's, The Stone, and the Mabuhay Gardens, and he knows where to score heroin—an important part of our friendship.

"We gotta get some cash," I say to no one in particular. Just thinking of dope has me jonesing, and I want more.

Lee's on the payphone, and I'm standing in the middle of Market Street's expansive brick sidewalk. People stroll by, and I know they got the cash I need, and I want to scream: *Hey, I'm a fucking starving artist, give me your money!* But instead I mumble, "Spare cigarette?" And this really cute girl stops and hands me a Virginia Slims Light. Which totally sucks and, yeah, I fucking hate Virginia Slims Lights, they're the longest most tasteless cigarettes ever made. But the girl is so goddamn cute, all I can say is, "Thanks."

"Chris gave me a plus one for tonight," says Lee. "What the hell you smokin', a tampon?"

Chris is the soundman at the Mabuhay Gardens, a punk club in the heart of San Francisco's strip joints and sleazy bars on Broadway. I don't know it then, but Chris and I are going to be best friends for the next ten years. Until Chris gets murdered and I slip farther into heroin's embrace, losing all sense of who I am.

But back then it's new and exciting, life's good and we never thought it would end. Chris introduces me to a girl named Bobby. I like her a lot and we start going out. Only Bobby doesn't tell me that Chris is her boyfriend, or rather, he was until I showed up. But I don't find this out until I move in with her and I'm thinking Chris is definitely going to kick my ass. Instead we become friends, all of us living together in a cramped North Beach apartment— one big happy post-nuclear punk family doing drugs and staying up all night.

Then I somehow land this dead-end day job stuffing envelopes for a corporate convention planner. From 9 AM to 5 PM I mindlessly fold registration forms and pamphlets and then cram them into mailing envelopes, run them though a postage machine, and stuff them into bags and drag them to the post office. Coffee breaks and lunch hours, I'm in the storage room with the rest of my part-time degenerate coworkers doing whatever drugs we can scam.

"Ever smoke Quaaludes?" asks Marsha, a nondescript girl who works in the copy room and has had sex with pretty much everyone in the office. Once a month we all get a memo that's a photocopy of her asshole and spread butt cheeks pressed against the glass of the Xerox machine.

"Why the fuck would I smoke Quaaludes?"

"There's kind of a rush, it's different."

"Just give me the fuckin' pill. You smoke yours."

And if that mundane existence alone was all that life offered there never would've been any question as to what drove me into being a dope fiend. Except, that job was just a bump in the road. I lived for the night and getting out to the club. And, thankfully, Chris would put me on the guest list for bands like the Avengers, the Mutants, Crime, Dead Kennedys, and DOA. Between shows I'd play pinball and get to know everyone who worked there. After a while the bartenders started flowing me free drinks. Then I figured out who the dealers were and spent most of my time shooting dope or snorting speed in the employees' permanently dirty bathroom down the hall behind the bar.

Saturday nights are usually really busy, and this one is no exception, so when one of the crew doesn't show up, Chris introduces me to Dirk Dirksen, the club's promoter. I've been introduced to Dirk about ten times, but he always acts like he doesn't know me—it's part of his demeanor, part of his caustic charm.

"Ever work stage?" says Dirk.

"Yeah," I lie.

"Just don't lose any fucking microphones."

Flipper is the headliner, and there's two other bands before them. Between sets I unload the previous band's gear, set up the mics and stands and run cords for the next band. Plugging in amps, miking the drums, and helping out with anything that needs getting done. When Flipper hits the stage I stand off to the side behind the bass amp and watch the chaos ensue. Their first notes are a guttural barrage, a bass-driven dirge that sends a mass of skinny kids in mohawks and leathers diving off the stage. While in the pit skinheads slam into each other, giving it the appearance of contact sports.

It's totally different being up on the stage. I get a rush from the energy. The PA pounding out the sound, the lights pulsing and glaring, the crowd staring at you, surging forward, and the band playing. Will Shatter, the lead singer, leans on the microphone stand, his eyes slits. He's in a nod. Holding up a beer, he invites the crowd to come on stage and sing with him. He's screaming, "I am the wheel!" swinging his arm around in a circle. I watch, mesmerized. The heroin-speed-alcohol combination has got a hold on me. I'm about as happy as I've ever been and I just want to go out there and sing with Will and have fun. And when some scrawny punker girl grabs the other vocal mic, unplugs it, and jumps back into the crowd with it stuffed in her pocket, I'm busy taking another hit off my beer and don't even notice.

"Not paying you shit for tonight," Dirk says. "You lost a mic. Told you not to."

The club closes. It's early morning, we're all heading out across deserted, fog-enshrouded Broadway Street, back to our apartment on Romolo Alley. Drinking beers we'd bought off-sale from the bar owner, Ness Aquino.

Our small one-bedroom apartment is packed full with mopey lead singers, guitar players, bartenders, junkies, strippers, roadies, transvestites, speed freaks, underage runaways, groupie girls, and hangers-on. Music blasts from the stereo, everyone's screaming, and no one is listening. The apartment reeks of cigarettes and spilled beer.

Our neighbors fucking hate us.

In the morning, after no sleep, or maybe a short nap I can't remember and definitely don't feel, I do a hit of speed in the bathroom and drag my ass downtown to my loser day job and watch the clock until it's time to go back and do it all over again.

"You a punk rocker?" Isabella asks. I have the biggest crush on her, but I've never said a word in her direction. Her life is salsa dancing, soul music, and lowriders. She lives in the Mission. We've worked together for a year now and this is the first time she's talked to me.

"Yeah, punk," I say.

"You guys really beat the shit outta each other on the dance floor?"

"I don't dance."

"You don't dance? Everybody fuckin' dances."

"I do heroin," I say, and her eyes go wide.

When Dead Kennedys come looking for a soundman to take on tour, they hire Chris. On Chris's recommendation, Microwave—their road manager—hires me as a roadie, and I quit my day job. On the nights the band plays out of town, I get paid twenty-five dollars. Which immediately goes to buying drugs, and I'm always broke. But the band has three cases of beer on their rider. And instead of eating I drink beer and scam whatever shitty bar food there is at the venue.

But the Kennedys, especially Jello Biafra, really don't do drugs. They barely drink, and so I have to keep my habit on the down-low. And other than OD'ing in New York at the Algonquin Hotel, and some weird Valium/Placidyl mix-up in Omaha, I pretty much keep it under wraps.

Between Kennedy tours Chris starts working for T.S.O.L., a band out of LA, and I get a gig as their roadie. And it's a whole fucking other scene with everyone getting high. And now, not having to hide it, my using increases, and the more dope I shoot, the less I care about anything—except shooting more dope.

It's the middle of summer, hot as hell. T.S.O.L.'s doing a gig at the Rock Hotel in New York City. I've been out all day, scoring and shooting the China white dope you buy in little glassine bags on the streets of the Lower East Side. I'm totally loaded, but I'm still up on stage, working the show.

"You're fuckin wasted," yells Mitch Dean, the drummer, as he throws a stick at me.

"So?" I say, and stumble off behind the side-fills and nod out.

In the middle of a song Ron Emory's guitar cord gets yanked out, twisted up around the foot of a stage diver, and I get it untangled and try to plug it back in. But I'm standing three feet away from Ron, nodding, my eyes barely open, with the cord in my hand while everyone's yelling.

Between those two bands we're constantly out on the road. And since we're gone all the time, that girl Bobby that Chris and I live with, she loses interest and starts fucking Will Shatter from Flipper, going so far as to move him into our apartment. I come home and have nowhere to go, and end up sleeping on friends' couches. I eventually hook up with Alicia and move in with her at Mission A, the notorious punk-rock house on Mission Street. Which is good and bad, as I have a place to stay, but when Alicia and I are together all we do is fuck, shoot dope, and make our lives miserable—it's Sid and Nancy all over again.

And Chris, having nowhere to live, gets tired of SF and moves to LA, telling me to come down. There are lots of bands and clubs to work at. But I don't want to leave Alicia. And I'm too strung out.

Then I get my first real break. Getting hired as the road manager for the UK band Subhumans. They came over from England with just a guitar and a bass and we borrow gear for every goddamn show all the way across country. I'm the only one who can legally drive and I end up driving the entire tour, not sleeping for days. I do a lot of drugs and drink way too much. Half out of my mind most of the time, I barely remember what fucking city we're in. When the tour ends in New York, I drop the band off at JFK and realize I'm three thousand miles away from home. It takes me three days, driving nonstop without any drugs, to get back to SF.

Whenever I return off tour it's always bittersweet. Usually I have no money—every cent having been spent on dope. And worse, Alicia is usually in debt to every dealer she knows. Yet I'm still fucking stoked to be home with my girlfriend, sleeping in my bed and eating food. But just like Martin Sheen's character Willard said in *Apocalypse Now*, "When I was home after my first tour, it was worse. I'd wake up and there'd be nothing... When I was here, I wanted to be there; when I was there, all I could think of was getting back...I wanted a mission, and for my sins, they gave me one...and when it was over, I never wanted another."

And I guess, perhaps for my sins, Flipper hired me as road manager on a horrific winter tour across the US in their International Harvester bread truck. It was freezing and the heater didn't work—all of us bundled up in overcoats taking turns at the wheel, endless nights of driving highways, crisscrossing frozen fields and the prairies of America.

This was my life for five years. It was the best. The most amazing, exciting time to be young and strung out and involved in something so creative and powerful. To have a best friend like Chris and work together doing something I loved. Up on stage every night, watching the show, seeing performers like Will, who was also a friend. To be on the road, without a care, fucking a different woman in every city, buying new clothes when the old ones got dirty. A never-ending string of clubs, dressing rooms, motels, roadside diners, and truck stops, stretched out along miles of highways, interstates, and turnpikes.

"...and when it was over, I never wanted another."

The Kennedys broke up, Flipper dissolved, T.S.O.L. went missing in action, Chris was in LA, and I quit looking for other bands because I couldn't stop shooting dope long enough to care. Alicia and I finally managed to get ourselves kicked out of Mission A. Which was near impossible, as the place was full of drug addicts. Except anyone who came to see us somehow ended up OD'ing and everyone got sick of the cops and paramedics being there every night. So we moved, and Alicia tried to kill herself, and then I left to go to New York.

Reflections

Slouched down on a park bench in Midtown Manhattan, *it* was all coming back to me. Romancing that first hit on a joint I'd taken fifteen years ago, snorting coke off a mirror, Quaaludes by the handful, or beating that crusty gray cotton for the tenth time when I knew damn well there wasn't another hit left in the spoon. I loved drugs, and I thought they loved me, so maybe my present situation wasn't so bad. I was alive and well, after all, and so far able to afford my ever-increasing heroin habit.

But after a couple of futile-ass attempts at painting that rosy picture of my life, I was forced to look at the reality of it all. My money was dwindling, I had no fixed address, and the only person I had to rely on was myself. Yet the idea of being alone sent me into a place I hated to be; once again, there I was wishing I was still unspoiled and a bit naïve—not the jaded strung-out dope fiend I'd become.

Back when it really mattered, back when I actually thought about shit and agonized over whether or not everyone liked me, I was hoping that all of them considered me a lovable human being and not a dejected soul. Being loaded all the time gave me the luxury to not constantly stress about this. Yet there were still times I'd stare into the mirror and contemplate which one of my various freckles, wrinkles, scars, or flabby lumps had turned the world's love off, leaving me abandoned, unwanted and alone.

Ultimately I hated my body, hated the way I looked and how I felt others viewed me. This led to some odd behavior on my part, like avoiding being photographed by strangers, only exposing my left side to security cameras, and worse: all those sneaked peeks at my reflection in store windows, parked car windshields, and those unforgiving three-sided dressing room mirrors that sit off to the side of the men's clothing department in repressive institutions like Macy's and Sears.

In reality, I hadn't even realized I was doing any of those things, as I was still mired in fears, honed by all the finely tuned phobias I'd harvested from adolescence. Now, as I sat uncomfortably on a dark green bench on one of those weird traffic-island kind of parks that grow right out of Broadway, the taxis rushing by in a stream of yellow, none of this seemed even the slightest bit relevant and all I could think about was scoring more dope and going home to shoot it.

Standing up, I stretch my right hand to flag a cab and can't help but notice my reflection, an unflattering somewhat bloated shape, in the darkened plate-glass window of the restaurant across the street. Just the sight of my body can give me the creeps, and I try to avoid looking at it whenever I can. "You fat slob," I whisper to myself, and then close the taxi door and give the driver a destination in the Lower East Side.

"Fuck I'm tired," I mumble, rubbing my eyes as I try to remember what time I'm to meet Paco, whether it was supposed to be 11 AM or later. *How the hell should I know? I can't even remember if today's today.*

"Hey, buddy, mind if I take Fourteenth?"

"Just get me there," I say, and as the taxi shimmies and shudders its way across four lanes of traffic, the reflection of my face in the passenger window stares back at me.

"Ugly mutha-fucker," I mumble. Only the driver hears me and I look up to see his eyes, or actually their reflection, looking in my direction. *Gotta remember to stop blurting things out.*

"Sorry, wasn't talking to you," I announce, making sure I'm actually saying the words out loud and not just thinking them. I fumble in my coat pocket for a cigarette only to remember that I smoked the last one twenty minutes ago.

"No offense taken," the cab driver says before turning his head in my direction. "Sir, may I ask you a rather personal question?"

"Well, if it's about anorexia, prenatal sex, osteoscopic surgery, Major League Baseball, the whereabouts of my mother, dental hygiene, IV drug use, adult inertia, or the use of certain trans fats as oil substitutes in most of America's favorite snack foods, well, then the answer is no. And I do reserve the right not to answer any inquiries on numerous other as of yet unnamed subjects."

"That mean yes?"

"Fire away, my good man. Fire away."

"Are you that funny guy from the television?"

"Who?'

"You know, the one that plays the space alien on that sitcom?"

"Ah, no."

"Are you sure?"

"Actually I have no idea what you're even talking about."

"Oh, I get it."

"You get what?"

"You don't want anyone to know it's you. Don't worry, I won't tell. Besides, who am I gonna tell?"

"Honestly, I'm not who you think I am."

"You look like 'im."

"I'm not him."

"You sound like 'im."

"I'm not him!"

Goddamn, ain't this a bitch? Every so often someone thinks they know me, thinks I'm that comedian, or some other actor. I've got a face that's familiar. Don't know why. But it is. It's kind of fucked to be taken for some celebrity, especially some sitcom comedian, when the truth is there's nothing funny about the whole goddamn thing and deep down inside I'm wishing I'd be mistaken for some rock star or at least a really cool artiste. But no, it has to be a TV actor. Fucking cursed, doomed to a life of being ugly, unloved, and resembling brand-name television celebrities. Still, makes me think I could have been something else in life, something other than a dope fiend. But as soon as those first nasty bits of withdrawal come rolling into my body, thoughts of that nature generally dissipate rather quickly and I'm back here: chasing the bag, getting high.

Just past the Bowery on Houston lies a derelict piece of cement and dead grass that carries the large and somewhat prestigious misnomer Sara Delano Roosevelt Park. But nobody ever calls it that. It is just referred to as the Park, as in "I'll meet you at the park." It's where I meet Paco to buy a bindle of dime bags filled with China white heroin, lactose, fentanyl, and assorted barbiturates—not necessarily in that order. The deal is I get ten bags for the price of eight and then one of the bags is always empty, so in reality I get nine. Which is kind of an outright New York payoff, only I don't get to tip the dealer myself. Not unlike having the gratuity already added on to the bill at a high-class restaurant.

I see the edge of the park come into view. "It's there on your right," I tell the driver and hand him some cash as he pulls over. The bright morning sun makes for a mirror-like reflection on the window and I try not looking at myself and step out of the cab. When I close the door and turn around I notice the park is empty except for a bum or two sleeping on one of the various decrepit benches. Alone and slightly dope sick I stare off into space, wondering if I'm early or late. There's not a working payphone within at least a good quarter mile and calling Paco is out of the question. So I stand there wondering what to do. Then a man stumbles out of the tavern across the street and it's obvious.

The bar smells of stale beer and dirty carpets mixed with crushed cigarette butts. From the looks of this place, it's one of those dives that should be called Joe's or Lou's, but I didn't bother to check the name before I came in. A long bar runs the length of the room with a few booths off to the right and then what looks like a very well-worn pool table sits in the back under a hanging lamp.

"Got a payphone?" I ask the lumpy-headed cross-eyed guy who's standing behind the bar.

"Phone fur payin' cussamers only."

"Okay, jeez already. Give me a fuckin' beer and then point me in the direction of the phone."

"Milla, Bud, McSorley, Guinea?"

"What?"

"Wha kinda beer youse wan?"

"How about one that you pour into a glass and it foams a little?"

"That I kin do."

Next to the pool table is one of those payphones from back in the days when a call only cost a dime and I'm almost surprised to see that there's not a dial.

"¿Hola?"

"Is Paco there?"

"¿Paco? ¿Paco quién? ¿Quién llama?"

A television blares away on the other end and I can hear the woman breathe as she awaits my response. I don't know exactly what to say to convince her that Paco needs to talk with me. Because right now it's of the utmost importance and I'm without a single phrase of Spanish to woo her confidence. "Senoro, I needa speak wit Paco, el vantay!"

From behind me I hear someone clear their throat and then say, "It doesn't help to try and imitate a Puerto Rican accent, man."

Paco walks up to me dressed in what looks like a New York Yankees uniform made of silver lamé. He needs no more advertisement that he's a drug dealer than that suit. Three gold strands I've undoubtedly paid for hang round his neck, and on his left wrist, loose to the point of almost falling off, hangs a matching gold Rolex. On his feet: bright red alligator-skin Adidas.

"Why you white dudes always think if you affect a Spic accent it'll get you in good with the dope man?"

I hang up the phone, doing a little shake of my head that I'm certain would look cool if I were a badass gangbanger, or at the very least wasn't a hundred-and-twenty-pound spike-haired junkie trying to cop dope in a dark empty bar. Walking back to my barstool I catch a glimpse of myself in the mirror behind the liquor bottles and immediately make a mental note of what a fat slob I am and unenthusiastically sit down in front of my beer.

"How you find me, man?" I ask and then take a sip of beer.

"Word on the street is some skinny-assed dope-fiend-looking white dude just got outta a taxi and beelined it for this bar. Hell, man, you know that this is my neighborhood. So now that we've established the fact that you're here and that I'm here, what can I do you for my man?"

Taking another sip off my beer, I lower my right hand under the bar and ease a small roll of money out of my pants pocket. A hundred and sixty is the price for two bindles. Being that dope fiend that wants to get the most for his money, I got a hundred and forty-two. All neatly rolled up with twenties on the outside so it looks fat like all the money's there. Paco knows I'm going to short him, and I know he's going to short me the usual amount. That's just the way things work.

"Gimme two, and could you not short me this time? Like to get what I pay for," I tell him, and then involuntarily do that little shake of the head thing again.

"Is the money right?"

"Right as it always is."

"Sure you right, baby."

The bags, the money, they all transact in a quick handshake and Paco nods farewell and I go back to my beer, the dope now safely hidden away, burning a hole in my pocket. The question is: do I walk the four blocks to the crib or try and do a quick shot in the men's room?

Looking up, I see the bartender staring at me with his deadpan cross-eyed expression. Forget the men's room, this dude already knows what I'm about. So I pat the two bindles of dope sitting in my pocket like talismans and get up off the barstool to leave.

Some dope fiends, they're cool once they score their drugs, withdrawal's all but gone, they're almost physically well just having the dope in their hands. But I'm not like that, never have been.

A block and a half later I'm standing in front of Sal's pizzeria, taking a breather, and out comes Mikey. I'd guess I'd call him a friend or maybe it'd be a little more on the real side to just say that at times we've shot some dope together.

"Yo, man, got a cigarette?" he says.

"Nah, Mikey. I'm out."

Mikey looks terrible, looks like somebody just ran over his dog. Then again, Mikey always looks like that, with this Bon Jovi New Jersey rocker persona that he's been slowly cultivating into New York street junkie chic.

"Did ya hear 'bout me an' Darleen?" he asks and then stands there blocking my way, waiting for me to respond.

Darleen is Mikey's girlfriend, been going out for years—one more depressingly cute junkie couple living in the Lower East Side. Mikey always has a story about him and Darleen, and it usually ends up in tragedy with them losing their dope or getting evicted and then Mikey uses it as an excuse to put the touch on people, asking for money. But today it ain't like I got time to listen or even any money to lend to pay for their habits instead of mine. Yet, for some reason, I still say, "No, man. What happened?"

"Things been goin' bad, stayin' at the hotel, don't got no money. Seems like it ain't gonna get no better. So we decided to end it all last night, man. Went to the dope man, gotta few bindles an' said we was goin' out. Made up our minds, man. Fuckin' life sucks."

Mikey was drunk or high on dope or wasted on pills. I could barely understand him, and he was seriously cutting into my getting-high time. With a wave of my hand I urged him on, trying to get him to tell me the rest of his story even if I didn't believe it.

"Well, like I said, we're stayin' at the hotel, so we got up in the room an' Darleen, she cooks it into two rigs. One fer me, one fer her. An' then she says we gotta do it all at once an' OD in each other's arms. Only she said to make it legit, really do it right, we gotta write a note 'bout how we can't take livin' like this no more, how we hate this world an' how we're in too much pain to continue on. She says that when they find us it'll make it that much better—really show 'em sumpin. So I write the note sayin' all this shit she toll me to say—an' then we shoot the dope—best high I had all year. Only I wake up this mornin' and Darleen don't."

"Jesus, Mikey," I say, when I finally realize what he's trying to tell me. "Man, are you all right?"

"Fuckin' weirded me out, it did. What wit' Darleen layin' there all blue an' me sick as a dog. Beat the cottons an' got well. Then I saw that goddamn note sittin' there an' it hit me like I was gonna be in trouble or sumpin. Crossed out all the we's an' changed them to I's an' stuck it back in her hand an' left wit out sayin' goodbye. Damn, dude. What I'm gonna do now?"

It sucks when I can't even empathize with my friend's pain. It sucks when I really just want him to go away so I can go get loaded by myself and don't have to share any of my dope with him. It sucks that the entire time he's been talking my reflection in the window of the dry cleaner behind him has absorbed all my attention and I just can't help looking at myself and thinking how fat I look. Mikey's lips are moving and he's saying something about being on his own and needing a place to stay.

"Sorry, Mikey. I gotta go. I'm late," I mumble and then leave him there standing with his mouth wide open as I cruise down the block heading for Elizabeth Street. I hate it when people do that kind of shit to me, ignore my misery and make some lame-ass excuse just to get rid of me. But I had to do it, otherwise Mikey'd be tailing me around all day whining about Darleen and

I really don't need to think about anything like that while I'm trying to get high.

And that's precisely why I don't hang out with girls like Darleen. Who needs the drama? I'm perfectly capable of cultivating one-sided unhealthy relationships with women who don't use drugs, are somewhat stable, and go to work every day while I lounge around their apartments "looking" for work. Besides, if Darleen wasn't busy contemplating suicide then she was cheating on Mikey or stealing his drugs. I couldn't take that kind of rejection all the time. Hell, Mikey's better off without her. With Darleen gone, it's one less arm to feed.

When I get to Elizabeth Street I'm almost to the apartment and I pick up the pace. A couple of the local dealers stand in front of the bodega and as I pass they ask me if I'm looking. Never buy dope right in front of your house. It's too close to home and then everyone knows your business. Besides, these guys use and they cut the shit out of their drugs, so buying from them is a total waste of time.

"Naw, I'm cool," I tell them and then cross the street to enter Dee's apartment building. As I walk up the stairs to the fifth floor, I'm bombarded by the stench of mildew, bug spray, and something that vaguely smells like someone is dead. Although I know Dee's not home, I knock just to be sure. Dee's sort of like my girlfriend. We've been hanging out together, drinking in bars when she gets off work, eating dim sum on Sunday, her only day off. She's got no idea that I'm shooting dope. She's got no idea that I've got a girl in California waiting for me to come home. She's got no idea of half the shit I'm up to. But she still gave me the keys to her apartment and so I live there, and while she's at work I shoot dope and when she gets home I tell her I've been busy looking for work. We both know it's a lie, but it doesn't matter. Then we go out to the bar and drink.

Even though I'm alone, I still lock the door to the bathroom before getting out the syringe and spoon I've stashed under the sink. The bindle of drugs feels weighty in my pocket as I pull it out and remove two of the glassine bags and carefully empty them into the spoon. Holding the rig in one hand, I turn the cold water on with the other, filling the cup that's at the edge of the sink. With the tip of the needle in the glass, I draw water into the rig and then press it back out onto the dope in the spoon. With the back end of the rig's plunger, I mix the dope into the water and then, shakily, hold the spoon out with one hand while applying the lighter's flame underneath.

A slight chemical smell hits the air. My stomach tightens. Pulling a Q-tip out of the medicine cabinet I tear off a small piece of the cotton and drop it into the cooked dope. Then, using the cotton as a filter, I press the tip of the needle into it as I draw up the liquid into the syringe. A quick tap to see if the air bubbles are gone and I'm looking around for something to tie off with, something I can use as a tourniquet around my arm and make my tired, overused veins stick out like they used to so that I can stick the needle in and get this dope inside of me.

Lying on the floor is a pair of Dee's pantyhose. I grab them, wrap them around the top of my right arm, flex the muscle, pump my fist. Halfway down, in the center, in the crook of my arm, a dark blue-green vein stands out and I press the needle into it. A line of blood shoots into the syringe's barrel as I register the vein; I push the plunger down while letting the pantyhose loosen as I finish, pulling the rig out of my arm. A trail of blood forms and runs onto the white tile floor.

There's that unmistakable taste in the back of my throat. There's that inviting warmth invading my entire body. My face itches, my stomach tightens, and then I'm calm and everything's all right. Eyes half closed, I'm thinking about a cigarette. Wrapping up my rig and spoon in the washcloth, I stuff it back up under the sink and look into the mirror. Staring back at me, eyes pinned, like I'm looking through a haze, I see someone who appears to be normal who looks a hell of a lot like me. Strangely, nothing about how I look or what I appear to weigh bothers me. I know I'm skinny, I know I'm attractive. Yeah, I know the whole world loves me, really they do.

I unlock the bathroom door about to leave and remember the blood on the floor. I carefully clean it up with the pantyhose and then stuff them into the garbage can by the sink. In the living room I notice the full-length mirror I turned around this morning before I went out and I turn it so the reflecting side is now showing. Face to face with my reflection I look at myself while I push my stomach out, trying to get it to go over my belt so I can see what a fat man really looks like. My torso's the size of most people's thigh; my legs in these pegged-legged jeans look like black pipe cleaners. The skin on my face almost seems transparent; the tracks on my arms stand out like dark bruises on my pasty white skin. I turn my face, catching my profile, and I know that I look good.

In the kitchen I grab a beer out of the refrigerator and walk into the bedroom and sit down on the bed with my back against the wall. September is ending. That sunshine I saw today was weak and winter is soon approaching. A junkie never gets warm during a New York winter and I shiver thinking about it. When I close my eyes, I can see California and I know I'll be going there soon.

THE ENTERTAINMENT CAPITAL
OF THE WORLD

LOS ANGELES, JULY 7, 1990

I'm knocking on the front door to the apartment, but no one is answering. It's 11 AM, the time I normally get here and wake Chris up so we can start the day, shoot some heroin, and begin selling dope to all the junkies whose phone numbers are continually flooding our pagers.

After another ten minutes of knocking and waiting, I walk downstairs, go around to the garage and make sure Chris's car is there—and it is. Back on the second-floor landing I knock once more. A small latched peephole opens and Chris's face appears behind the security grill.

"Who's there?" he asks, which is weird as we're eye to eye and I'm staring right at him.

"It's me," I say, and crush out a cigarette with the heel of my boot.

"Who's me?"

"Jesus Christ. It's fuckin' me. Me, as in Patrick, your fuckin' partner. Gonna let me in or what?"

Chris closes the peephole and I wait. Then there's the sound of a power tool, a drill maybe. The door is shaking and there's screeching noises added to the whir of the small motor.

When the door finally opens I walk in and find Chris, cordless drill in hand, sort of stooped over, dazed. On the floor are several three-inch screws he'd removed from where he'd obviously used them to hastily secure the door to the frame.

"What's up, man? You okay?"

"Fuck, dude. You should have been here last night."

"Why?" I say. "What happened?"

"Cops, man. I was surrounded."

Chris is making me nervous. I leave him there and wander around the apartment checking the different rooms, seeing if everything is secure. Near every window there's a pile of cocaine, a syringe, spoon, glass of water, and a gun. All the curtains have been drawn shut, and the rest of the drugs, money, scale, and paraphernalia are in a heap on the bed.

"Something happen last night?" I ask.

Chris closes his eyes and leans against the wall. When he swallows it appears to take a lot of effort. He's tired. He's wasted. He's been up all night shooting coke and he's past paranoid; he's bordering on deranged.

From the looks of things Chris had posted up all night at different windows shooting coke: the curtains slightly parted, his finger on the trigger, while hallucinating squadrons of police through blurry eyes.

He feebly gestures toward the window at the end of the hall. "They were in the trees."

Outside the window I see trees that are young saplings, no more than two inches in diameter. There is no way a small child could climb them without them breaking in two, let alone a fat-assed cop shinnying up to spy in our second-story windows.

"I saw 'em out there. Asked what they was doin'. The fuckers wouldn't answer."

"You actually saw them?"

"Then they're at the front door. Arguing about kicking it in. Arguing for hours. Sounded like a platoon."

I'm starting to worry. If there is one thing I know about the Los Angeles Police Department, it's they don't argue for hours about knocking down a dope dealer's door. They just do it. They come in guns blazing, kicking ass, and, if at all, ask questions later.

"Let's shoot some heroin, man. You need to chill out."

I fix it up and we both do our hits. The dope is good. I gave Chris extra—the dude definitely needs it. Even though I feel the shot, I'm wishing for a stronger rush. But I sit down and go with what I got and slowly nod into thoughts of how I got here and all that's happened.

Coming home to San Francisco from New York hadn't worked out. Alicia was clean and sober and going to meetings and I wasn't. Thinking I could get back into the music business while avoiding Alicia's newfound life of sobriety, I moved to LA and hooked up with Chris. But I was a fucking mess. Trying to stay clean, I still ended up chipping—shooting dope every once in a while. But I kept looking for work and finally got hired working stage for a production company that put on shows at clubs like the Palladium, the Palace, and the country club out in Reseda. In the afternoon I'd lug gear and set up the PA. Then I'd pretty much get high until it was time to load out. But my heart really wasn't in it. And I was bored.

Then Mike Roche, a good friend of ours and bass player for T.S.O.L., asked Chris to manage his dope business while he was on tour. Chris pulled me in and we started selling heroin in Hollywood. Our customers were all the wannabe rock-and-rollers, has-beens, and those currently on their way up. We'd score our dope in Long

Beach from Latino gangbangers and then sell it to all the white kids who were either afraid to go to the Mexicans or didn't know how.

The business grew and we never gave it back. Which was fucked. Like I said, Mike was a friend of ours. But the lure of dope and money was too much as we went from small packages to moving weight. Our pagers were constantly going off with people screaming for more. After midnight I had to turn mine off or it would buzz all night.

Every morning we'd hook up at Chris's apartment, shoot dope, and then deliver all over Hollywood. Driving all day from one end to the other. Answering the pager. Setting up meets. Stopping off for a quick shot. And then down to Long Beach to re-up.

The production company would call asking if I wanted to work and I'd turn them down, as I was making twice the money selling dope, and my drugs were paid for. As more and more people started buying from us and the business got larger, I stopped doing anything else.

While our business grew, so did the dangers. Several times we'd go to a delivery and sketchy-assed dope fiends would be waiting in the shadows trying to rip us off.

I step out of the car. The grocery store's parking lot is practically deserted. I'd told the new customer to meet us here at 8 PM. It's fifteen after, and I'm not used to junkies being late. It's usually the other way around, us rolling up and them bitching about how long they've been waiting.

"Gonna get something to drink," I say to Chris, then walk into the store.

As I come back out with a can of Coke, a skinny guy in a leather jacket and torn Levi's standing by a gumball machine says,

"Got the shit, dude?" He's in the shadows and his long stringy hair almost hides his face.

I start to reach into my pocket when he pulls a knife and lunges at me. I turn away just as the knife blade misses my throat. Stumbling backward I drop the can of Coke, then regain my footing and start running to the car as Chris cranks the ignition.

"What the fuck!" I yell. "Jesus, did you see that nut job?"

Chris fishtails the El Camino out into the street. I turn, trying to catch a glimpse of the skinny guy, memorize what he looks like, but there's no one there. "That's it, dude—we're getting guns."

After that everything went up a notch. Almost getting stabbed made it obvious there were consequences and possible repercussions that we hadn't even really considered. This affected how we dealt with customers. We trusted no one. And that's when Chris started changing. Getting really greedy and power-hungry, doing a lot of coke and leaving the deliveries to me. Then I'd get back and he'd demand the money, like he didn't trust me.

Slouched down in the chair, I'm still thinking I should've given myself the same amount as I gave Chris, as I'm not feeling it like I should. But maybe that's just due to the residual stress from last night's events and Chris's recent craziness. He's lying on the bed with his eyes closed, almost as if he's going to sleep. I can hear the pagers, they're vibrating on the desk, both been going nonstop for the last hour—hungry junkies looking for their morning fix.

"Dude," I say, "we gotta get going, there's money to be made."

Chris doesn't answer. He's either passed out or too out of it to respond. I reach over the desk for the chunk of black tar dope and break off a piece and put it in the spoon. When I'm just about done cooking it with the lighter, I grab a cigarette to use a piece of the filter as a cotton.

"Wha the fuck'er you doin'?" Chris slurs.

"Cooking a little more. Gave you over half, didn't feel mine."

"Fuckin' stealing from me."

"What?"

"You're always fuckin' stealing from me."

"Dude, I'd never steal from you."

Chris gets up off the bed, but he can barely stand. He weaves across the room and grabs the chunk of heroin and slumps down in the other chair by the desk.

"You want more? Here."

Yanking off a gram-size piece he throws it at me, then another, and another, and another. They're landing on the shag carpet, or on me, or on the desk. And every time he yells, "Here!"

I try to concentrate on drawing up the dope from the spoon into the rig, but one bounces off my forehead and I get pissed.

"Fuck you, dude!"

"Fuckin' thief," says Chris.

"That's it. Fuck you, man. I'm done. Call me when you stop being a fuckin' asshole. And quit shooting all that goddamn coke."

I throw the full rig on the desk, knocking over the spoon, and storm out of the apartment. Slamming the front door with its new screw-hole scars and chipped paint.

I didn't know that would be the last time I saw Chris, though I did talk to him twice after that. One night about six months later, I got a call. He was in a hotel in Glendale geeked out of his mind on coke and wanting me to come over. He was trying to make amends but I was still pissed and told him I couldn't come. I was in bed with Janus, my girlfriend, and didn't want to get up and deal with his insanity.

Another night I was dope sick, lying around the apartment, and he called.

"Hey, what's been going on?"

"Not a whole lot," I said.

"I've been thinking about, ah, you know."

"Yeah?"

"Wondering how shit got so fucked up?"

"I don't know, man. I don't know."

"Miss you riding shotgun, man. Just ain't the same. How 'bout I come by tomorrow, get you high?"

"Man, you can't do it now? Could really use it."

"Can't, but maybe tomorrow. Look, I'm dealing with a new connect out in Long Beach. Not trusting anybody right now. Maybe you take a ride down there with me in the morning?"

"All right, man. In the morning then."

"Later."

Two days later a railroad crew in Ontario, California, came across a metal storage trunk laid across the tracks. Inside was Chris's folded dead body. Put there like someone had hoped a train would run him over. The following morning it was in all the newspapers and on the news. After the first ten calls I stopped answering.

Two Ontario homicide detectives showed up at my door the next day. They flashed their badges and introduced themselves. Said they wanted to talk with me, but not here. I got in the back of their unmarked car and they drove me for an hour and a half across LA county out to the morgue in Ontario.

I'd been in hospitals and funeral homes, but I'd never been to a morgue. The place reeked of decay and disinfectant. Several covered bodies on gurneys lay stacked in a dark hallway. The overhead lights flickered as the cops led me through a maze of rooms.

Nobody had said a word since we got there, and I worried I was going to be arrested. When we finally got to the viewing room, a man in a white lab coat opened the door.

"Ready?" asked the man as he pulled off the sheet.

Chris's body lay prone on the steel gurney. His skin had turned a pale gray-blue, offsetting his tattoos. His blond hair was matted against the wound on his head. Cuts covered his entire body. His eyes were open, but he was dead.

As we stood over him, the two cops told me they knew all about us selling dope. Said they suspected me of killing Chris to control the business. I stared at Chris's caved-in skull and multiple stab wounds and felt strangely too numb.

"Go fuck yourselves," I said.

Another week went by before two more detectives came to my apartment.

"We know you were in business with Chris," one of the cops said. "You're still a suspect in his death."

"Only we're willing to forget that," said the other one, "if you tell us who your customers were."

The first one pulled out a notebook and pen like I was going to start blurting out names.

"We want everyone you sold to. We already know the connection, it's not as if we're asking for him. So this should be easy."

The two of them sat there on the lumpy gray couch in my small Hollywood bungalow and talked all kinds of shit. Like they were doing me this huge favor. But what they never told me was that four months earlier Chris had gotten arrested in Long Beach, and when he was being booked he didn't have an ID and used my name instead of his. Having toured together for years, Chris and I both knew each other's personal information like social security and driver's license numbers so we could fill out the required paperwork for car rentals, hotels, or plane tickets if the other person wasn't there. Thankfully a mutual friend got in touch and told me about it, although he didn't know what the bust was for. I could only assume it was sales or possession. Yet, then, out on bail Chris never called to warn me, as he had no intention of going to jail. Apparently he didn't give a fuck if I took the fall.

Either these two jerk-off cops didn't know about the bust or they didn't care. Not saying a word, I just stared at them until they finally left.

But now I was totally screwed. With no job, no dealing, and no money coming in, I tried to stop shooting heroin. I'd do a cold-turkey kick and be back on the shit in less than twenty-four hours. Everyone told me to go see a Dr. Mark. Supposedly he had the "cure"—a Buprenorphine and Valium cocktail that cut the kick down to a bare minimum. And when I could scrounge enough money I'd sit in his waiting room with the rest of Hollywood's dope fiends: frizzy-haired heavy metalers, pretty-boy glam bands, bondage babe pin-up girls, and high-class hookers. But I was struggling still and didn't really want to stop, so it never really took. Just sort of slowed me down a bit.

Yet without a good steady connection, instead of just being able to do heroin, I had to improvise, and when none was available I shot speed, and Dilaudids, and took pain meds and tranquilizers, or whatever I could get my hands on. Only with no money and a large habit I slowly slipped into the usual dope-fiend behaviors to get more: writing bad checks, faking deposits with ATMs, and shoplifting. With incredible ease, I began making the transition to petty criminal, breaking into cars, and apartments, and even storage-space complexes. Selling whatever I could to dope dealers, fences, or at the pawn shops. I even held yard sales in front of my apartment with all the stolen goods.

Very quickly the people I had hung with when I first moved to LA, the musicians and people who worked in the music industry, started avoiding me. Having never fully gotten in good with the locals, I soon found myself even more of an outcast. Alone, I sought the company of other junkies, street dealers, petty thieves, and hookers who didn't care what I did as long as I was getting high. I started hanging out in the shittier sections of Hollywood. Doing all-nighters in shooting galleries and decaying squatters' apartments.

When I was home I had one eye pressed against a slit in the front window's curtains looking for cops while I fingered the snub-nosed .38 tucked in the belt of my jeans. I trusted no one. My girlfriend was fucking every dope dealer with a dime bag. My landlord was evicting me. Scumbags were trying to rip me off. The speed had me so paranoid that most of the time I couldn't even go outside.

But Chris's death really fucked me up and I started getting even more reckless. I thought nothing about scoring dope in the alleys of downtown LA or going up into the shooting galleries of Echo Park. Gangbangers didn't faze me. Everyone I hung out with had done time or was on their way back to prison. To support my habit I started doing more burglaries. I broke into apartments at night, even when the people were home. When I had no other means to score I'd drive down to MacArthur Park's all-night crack market and rip off dealers on the street. Nothing mattered. It all just got bleaker and I did more and more dope to make it okay.

It's a typical sunny Southern California afternoon. I'm in a bit of a hurry coming back from ripping off a drug dealer in Van Nuys.

Hardcore Mexicans that were for sure going to be looking for me the next couple of days. I glance in the rearview just as the Highway Patrol throws on his siren and red lights. I've a bunch of outstanding speeding tickets. I figure this fucking cop is going to arrest me and so I casually stuff my gun and the stolen drugs under the bench seat of my El Camino and pull over.

Five minutes into it and it's just like I expected, handcuffed and sitting in the back of the patrol car as the cop calls in a warrant check.

The cop looks out over the top of his mirror shades, checking out my chrome mags, blue pearlescent paint, and lowered chassis. "What year's the El Camino?"

"Seventy-nine," I tell him, but that's about as much conversation as we've got in us. We sit in silence as the computer starts churning out a massive amount of information: all my traffic warrants, Chris's Long Beach bust, another warrant for his gun possession, and then, finally, I come up listed as being deceased.

"Holy shit." The cop turns around and stares at me. "You ain't dead. How the fuck you do that?"

Chris's and my information had been mated together in the cops' main computers and now both of us were listed as dead.

"I ain't never seen any bullshit like this. I gotta take you in," says the cop.

For two days I sit waiting in a holding cell and they still can't figure it out. Everything's a fucking mess. They don't know whose warrants are whose, and they don't know which one of us got busted in Long Beach. But it's not until after they take my fingerprints that they're able to figure out I'm not Chris.

Sitting back in the holding cell, I'm watching a slice of Wonder Bread on a bologna sandwich curl up and dry. A detective from Long Beach stands at the bars. "I came up here to try and straighten all this crap out," he says. "But I take one look at you and know you're not the Patrick O'Neil I busted. Even if all you punk white boys do look the same."

An hour later a sergeant unlocks my cell and gives me back my property.

"You're under investigation. Don't leave town," he says.

I get my car out of impound and drive out into the parking lot, but I don't know where the hell to go, or what to do. I got a tank of gas, sixty dollars, a 9mm, and a bunch of stolen heroin. I slip the transmission into drive and cruise around trying to figure this shit out. When it starts to rain I use half my money and get a shitty hotel room on the edge of Culver City. Shivering from the cold, I turn on the wall heater and sit down on the bed. The gun, stuck in the back of my pants, digs into me and I pull it out. Almost mindlessly I pull back the hammer and put it in my mouth. The metal against my teeth hurts, the acidic taste of oil invades my gums. The wind's blowing, and I can hear rain against the window. I'm thinking I don't want to do this. I'm tired of guns, robberies, people looking to kill me. I'm tired of my friends dying. I don't want to be alone, or strung out, or wanted by the police. I just want it all to end. But not this way.

I put the gun down.

I need to get the fuck out of Los Angeles.

WAITING

I stare at each passing car. *Man, he's not coming. I know he's not.* The dark shapes of the surrounding buildings cast shadows as the weak winter daylight fights its way through the morning fog. It's cold, but the goose bumps still pull at my flesh. A sheen of sweat glistens on the side of my face and down my neck.

I light a cigarette and the rising smoke finds its way into my eyes and I wave it away with the other hand. There's a cramping knot in my stomach. Muscles twitching. My skin feels like it's about to shed. There's a dull throbbing in my temples, and the rancid taste of tooth decay and too many cigarettes fills my mouth. I look down at the sidewalk. Seems like I'm always looking at the fucking ground.

A well-dressed couple walks out from an apartment building. She smiles. They embrace. He touches her cheek with his hand and kisses her on the lips. She laughs, and mouths the words "I love you." He turns, walks up Haight Street. She teeters on high heels and stands next to me at the bus stop.

"Been waiting long?" she asks.

I want to slap that stupid look of love off her face, but I know she's just asking me about the bus. And, yeah, I'm standing here, but I'm not waiting for the bus. I've been waiting for the dope man for at least an hour. Fighting the urge to puke I fumble with my cigarette, flicking the ash and then take another drag. "There'll be a bus coming inna minute," I tell her. "There always is."

I look up, see Saul standing across the street. We've both been waiting. Posted up on either corner in case the dealer comes from a different direction and drives by without seeing us. Like anybody could miss two shivering junkies standing on a street corner frantically watching every car that drives by.

I take another hit off the cigarette and rub my hands together. A bus pulls up in front of me. The door opens and the heat from inside blows against my face. The woman, now behind me, waits for me to get on so she can follow.

"After you," I say, and step aside. I'd like to get on the bus. Sit in one of the front seats by the heater and drive away. But I'd still be dope sick, and then what the hell would I do? I take the last drag on my cigarette and toss it into the gutter. I wish I were home asleep in bed with Jenny—like always, she's there warm under the covers with the TV on, a forgotten cigarette burning away in the ashtray. I can barely pull that woman out of bed and here I am in the cold, waiting to score for the both of us.

Sucking in a blast of diesel exhaust as the bus pulls away, I stare through the brown haze and shrug my shoulders at Saul. He looks at me, rolls his eyes, and shakes his head. It's always like this when you're waiting for dope. Some times are worse than others. Depends on who's making the deliveries and how many junkies are ahead of you.

A small beat-up Toyota turns the corner. Two Latino-looking dudes are inside. I squint, trying to make out if I know them. There's always a distinct possibility of a new driver. The car cruises by. Its occupants don't even notice us. Just because they're Latinos doesn't mean they're delivering dope. I walk over to Saul.

"He's not coming, man."

"He's coming," he tells me.

Down the block a cheesy red and white Mustang turns the corner and drives toward us.

"It's him," I say.

"'Bout fucking time."

The Mustang pulls over. Saul jumps in and they drive a few yards before the car stops and Saul gets out. Without saying a word, we start walking toward Fillmore Street. We have to go to the café so Saul can go to the bathroom and split the piece of dope in half. He has to go to work. I have to go home. Jenny is waiting for me.

We walk past the housing project and the old, dilapidated Victorians of the Haight, the sidewalk crowded with winos, panhandlers, and yuppies on their way to work. At the bus stop a couple of women decked out in fashionable business attire and two men in suits eye us. Slouched against the bus shelter, reading a newspaper, a rather disheveled-looking hipster sucks on a cigarette and glances at his wristwatch.

I look at Saul. Saul looks at me. We both turn and stare at this guy's perfectly messed coif, his wrinkled tight black pants, jacket, and shirt with the right collar sticking up. There's a crude bluebird tattooed on his neck that's peeking out from the front of his shirt.

"Hey, ya gotta cigarette?" I ask him.

"Sure, man. How's it going, brother?"

I take the cigarette. Look the guy in the eye and start walking again. Everything about Saul and me is disheveled. All of our clothes are wrinkled, dirty, frayed. We look like junkies. We dress like junkies. We are junkies. That guy's eyes weren't even pinned—

he don't use dope. And besides, he was waiting for the bus with all the other working stiffs.

"You can't buy this look. You have to earn it," Saul sighs. And then he turns, goes into the café and I sit outside, smoking, waiting. Junkies, at least the majority of us, don't go to work. We don't have jobs. What Saul and I are doing this morning *is* our job. That Saul has a paying gig to go to today is nothing more than a fluke. He'd met some woman on Chestnut Street while panhandling and she'd hired him to make Chris Isaak dolls. Actually, they're puppets. Chris Isaak puppets. So it isn't even a real job. It's going to end soon, or Saul is going to screw it up. But for now it's our ticket for getting money.

I take a drag off my cigarette and watch the people walking by. I just can't comprehend being on my way to work. And what happens when you get there? What could you possibly do all day?

A barefoot woman wrapped in only a huge dirty brown parka walks toward me, asking for spare change with her hand out. There's a crazed look in her eyes, crud or scabs on her chin, and although she's walking slowly her movements are jerky, spastic. Almost robotic. She's definitely a crackhead, probably on her way back to the projects. You can't buy that look either.

And then Saul's standing next to me. He slips a crumpled piece of paper into my hand. My share of the dope.

"Come on. I gotta catch the streetcar," he says. "Come on. I'm late." And then he starts walking fast down Fillmore to the Church Street station. Saul has obviously smoked a hit in the bathroom. He's well. Ready for the day. I'm still a little stuck in the "I'm-gonna-fuckin'-puke" stage and dragging my ass behind him, trying to keep up. Besides, I don't smoke dope. I shoot dope. Smoking is a total waste of heroin.

"Got enough for one fare," Saul says as he counts the change in his hand. "So check it out. I get on the streetcar, get a transfer, and toss it out the window, you grab it and take the bus home. Okay? Come on. I gotta go, man." And with that he's up the steps of the waiting streetcar, paying the fare, pushing past the people at the front of the car.

The doors close, the streetcar begins to move. Just as it clears the platform a window opens, and a transfer flies out. A gust of wind catches the paper. It spirals up in the air, and then gets sucked down, vanishes under the streetcar.

I stand on the platform and watch as the streetcar becomes smaller and smaller and then disappears over the hill. I'm a half an hour away by bus from home. I have no money and no rig to shoot the dope that's in my pocket. I walk the half block back to the bus stop, staring at the ground for change, or another transfer. Five minutes later a bus pulls up. I wait by the back door. No one gets off. I stare at a woman through the window. Trying to will her to open the door. But she just stares back, a tired expression on her face.

The bus pulls away. I fumble with my pack of cigarettes and pull out the last one. Light it, toss the crumpled pack on the ground. Inhale and immediately a rush of hot slime explodes out of my mouth and nose, spraying the sidewalk at my feet. Wiping my face with the back of my sleeve, I swallow, breathe slowly, and stare at the concrete. A tough-looking old guy standing next to me moves over a few feet and pretends to look for the next bus.

Puking has become as natural as breathing. When you exist on heroin, cigarettes, candy bars, and the occasional cheeseburger, your stomach is always heaving shit back up. Only a shot of dope makes everything okay.

I glance up as a bus makes its way through the intersection and pulls to the curb. The back door opens, dislodging passengers. There's a lot of people getting on and off, keeping the driver's attention to the front of the bus. I slip in the back door and quickly sit down.

Twenty-five long agonizing minutes later the bus pulls over at my stop. As I get off, the cold wind hits me. My nose begins to run. I pull my jacket tight and start walking the three blocks to my apartment. I feel like I'm about to pass out. My eyes are watering. My fingers are numb.

At the alley door of my apartment building I fumble for the keys in my jacket pocket, but I'm shivering so bad I'm having trouble getting my fingers to close around them. Shaking, I push the doorbell and wait for Jenny to buzz me in. Seconds pass and then the electric latch hums and I'm in the alley walking under the back stairs to our basement apartment. In this neighborhood, they refer to places like ours as a garden apartment. If you were to walk past our front door, you'd end up in a small walled-in yard filled with withered and dying plants.

I push open the apartment door. The air is hot and stifling and smells of cigarette smoke as the gas heater blasts away in the corner. I walk across the living room, through the French doors, and into the bedroom, take off my jacket and toss it on a pile of dirty clothes.

Jenny's in bed, under the covers, the top of her head barely visible.

"What took you so long?" she asks.

"I thought he wasn't coming, then I lost Saul's transfer. Had to sneak on the fuckin' bus. Can you get some fresh water while I get the shit ready?"

"I'm too cold to get up again," she says, and then turns the covers down and looks at me as I sit on the bed. "You're not gonna use the water from last night are you?"

"Fuck, can't you do anything?" I say, and then stomp across the bedroom into the kitchen.

"I'm sick, baby." Jenny's large dark eyes and turned-down lips make that pleading helpless look she uses whenever she wants something.

"I know, babe. I'm sick too,"

When I get the dope unwrapped it looks really small. Just a tiny lump of black tar. Amazing, something this small gets both of us well. That all it takes is a half-full syringe of dirty water to make me feel halfway normal.

The smell of vinegar hits my nose as I run the lighter back and forth under the spoon. Inside, the lump of tar melts with the water ,forming an amber-looking liquid. Gently I put the spoon down, drop in a cotton, and then draw half the liquid into a syringe. With a belt tight around my arm I pierce the skin, hit the same vein I always use.

The warm rush takes me by surprise. The dope is good today. I rinse the rig three times, spraying the bloody water across the room toward the black drapes that cover the windows. Jenny moves closer to me. She's got the belt around her arm and holds it up to me as I draw the remaining dope into the syringe. Jenny's got girl veins. Tiny, small veins that are really hard to hit. She can't do it herself. I'm much more practiced than she is, so I do it for her. Yet most times, when the needle registers, and I think I'm in the vein, halfway through pushing the dope in, her arm swells up, the dope going into the muscle instead, and I have to find another vein to use.

I check her arm. Bruise marks and an old abscess that has only started to heal. I turn her arm toward the light and see a small blue vein by her elbow and stick the needle in. A weak trickle of blood enters the syringe and I start pushing down the plunger.

"Stop," she yells, tears in her eyes. "It fuckin' hurts. You're missing."

I take the rig out, pull the plunger back and push out the air bubbles. With my fingers I wipe the blood off her arm and feel around for another vein. Finding what looks like one, I put the needle back in and tug on the plunger, the blood runs in. I'm in a vein, and I start pushing the remaining dope into her arm.

"You're missing again," she cries. But by the time she says it all the dope is in her and I'm pulling the rig out. "You missed," she says, looking at me with sad, hurt eyes. She rubs her arm.

"Got a cigarette?" I ask and spray the curtain with the rinse water from her syringe.

She takes one and hands me the pack. I light mine and then hold the lighter for her. The cigarette tastes good, like nicotine candy. I pull off my shirt and push a pillow up against the back of the bed and lay down.

"Love you," Jenny says as she pulls the covers around her.

"Love you too, babe," I say, and then close my eyes. I can hear the patter of raindrops against the windows, the noise louder when the wind blows. It's cold and wet out there, and I'm warm and dry, and I've got dope in me. I take another drag on the cigarette, and roll over and put my arm around Jenny. I can hear her breathing. I can feel her thin body under my arm. I take another hit on the cigarette and then roll back over to my side of the bed and put it out.

Scratching my face, I try to remember what day it is, only I can't even remember the month. An image of a transfer swirling in the wind slips through my mind as a train slowly moves away and I find this funny. My stomach growls. I think of food. More heroin.

Another cigarette. I sink further into the bed. Leaning back I cover my eyes with my arm and let myself fade into a nod.

There's sun coming in through the windows of the house we used to live in on Mission Street. I'm warm and something feels good and Jenny is lying in my old bed, her breasts moving up and down, her mane of black hair splayed across the pillows. I can feel her tongue running along my chest. She grabs my arms and arches her back, her hair falls down around her shoulders. I'm kneeling in front of her. Her ass on my thighs, her legs, up in the air, the backs of her calves resting against my shoulders. I reach down and grab her hips and push myself into her. She's warm and slippery—everything that sex is supposed to be.

I've been awake for a couple of days. I'm numb and tired and I'm not sure if this is really happening. Two days shooting heroin and meth, taking Valiums, not sleeping, and not eating, and she comes to my room to say hi, and now we're in bed together, naked, having sex.

I've wanted to fuck Jenny ever since I met her. And tonight she's here and I run my hands along the backs of her thighs. Grab each of her ankles, push her legs down, slowly pull my cock out and push it back into her as deep as I can. Yet the meth, or lack of sleep, or both, is totally messing with me because it's as though I'm not fucking her. It's like I'm watching and feeling everything, but for some reason, I'm not actually here. As if any minute I'm going to regain consciousness and be alone in bed, and the whole thing some kind of drug-induced daydream.

My fingers move along her ankles. I caress her foot. Turn my head, and lick her heel, and then slip her toe in my mouth. She squirms and says it tickles. Letting go, I lean forward, pushing her legs back, my hands now wrapped around her ankles. She shoves herself against me, I push into her harder. Our breathing halted, shorter, she moans. I pull her hips forward, her legs slip to either side of me. She arches her back, her head lifts up off the pillow. I stiffen, hesitate, breath in, and then jerkily pull out. My cum shoots across her stomach. My arms hold me above her, my eyes half closed, an involuntary shudder across my shoulders. She grabs me by my neck, pulls me downward. I fall into her arms, my head rests on her shoulder. I'm out of breath.

Everything slows down, and my vision is blurry. I try to talk, but my mouth's too dry. I'm exhausted, warm, I just came, and don't want to move. I want to stay in bed, keep having sex, do more drugs. I really need a cigarette.

"Marry me," I whisper into Jenny's ear. She stops breathing, and then she laughs, pushes my head back away from her shoulder.

"Not now," she says. "Maybe in a year, or when we get to know each other, but not now."

"Whatever," I say. And then without moving off of her, I reach for the cigarettes. I don't want to let go of her. I already know we're not going to be together forever. But somehow I want to keep her with me. I roll over, lean back and light two cigarettes, hand one to Jenny. A cool move I've only seen in movies but never tried to actually do myself. She pulls the covers up around her and takes the cigarette.

That morning I'd driven Jenny to her first class at City College. I didn't know what class she was taking or why she was even going to school, as she didn't seem to be all that excited about the whole thing. When I stopped in front of the school's parking lot to drop her off, she mumbled something about how she'd rather spend the day with me, and then pushed against the car door getting ready to get out. Turning her head, she leaned back in and kissed me on the lips, smiled—our first kiss. As I watched her walk away, I felt something inside of my chest sort of twist.

My last relationship had ended rather badly—more of the same old shit. Girl meets guy, guy gives her heroin, girl turns into crazed drug addict, and the relationship goes to hell as the dope takes over. But the really stupid part, the unexplainable insanity, was that I was still in love with her. Even after all the bullshit. The cheating. The lying. Treating each other like strangers who fuck once in a while. And still being angry and hurt, I was scared of going through it all again with someone else.

Only, I didn't want to be alone anymore. And Jenny didn't come off as hard or as jaded as the rest of the women I'd known. Yet, I knew she wasn't innocent. In my mind I was making her out to be this perfect little girl that was all in love with me because I was this amazing dude, doing amazing things.

I knew she'd been in some trouble. Her uncle, a former friend of mine and the manager of the building I lived in, had moved her in as a favor to his sister, Jenny's mother. A few times Jenny and I had run into each other in the building's hallway, and then when I was selling some drugs to Sweet, Jenny had been there and we finally talked. She was flirtatious, smiled and laughed at every stupid thing I said. When I asked her why she moved here she told me her boyfriend had recently left her and after that everything had gone bad. Stuck in some rundown apartment complex on the beach, she'd done too much speed and watched the crows as they careened across the sky. In a vacant lot by the side of her building she'd found some sort of Voodoo shrine and thought maybe she was possessed.

I watched her lips move as she talked and wanted to know what it felt like to kiss them. Yet I couldn't picture this beautiful girl doing all the crazy shit she said she was doing. A short time later we started hanging out together, and not much longer after that we were inseparable—the two of us against the world.

Somewhere there's a phone ringing, and it pulls me out of my half-conscious memories. I sit up, answer it, and grab the cigarettes. It's Saul on the other end. Says he's getting off work early. The woman only needed him for a few hours. But she pays cash, so he's got money, enough for dope. I tell him I'll meet him back up in the Haight.

The clock says I've been out for two hours. Jenny's next to me, wrapped in covers, breathing slow. I touch her warm body and run my hand along her ass, but she's asleep and doesn't move. I get up and take the spoon with the dope residue into the bathroom to try and get what's left in the cotton. I know there's nothing there. But sticking a needle in my arm always makes me feel better.

Back in the bedroom I light a cigarette and search the pile of dirty clothes for bus fare. Pulling on my shirt, I shake Jenny and tell her I'm leaving.

"Where ya going?" she asks.

"I'm meeting Saul."

She sits up and reaches for the pack of cigarettes. "We're almost out," she says, and waves the half-empty pack at me. I reach over, take two smokes and slip them into my shirt pocket.

"I'll try and score a pack while I'm out."

"Did you eat today?"

I look down at her and try and calculate how I'm going to get cigarettes and food with no money. "I'll see what I can do," I mumble.

"Be careful." She reaches over to turn on the television. Jenny can sit all day watching TV. Waiting for me, waiting for the dope—waiting for whatever she thinks is coming her way.

Saul's standing on the corner when I get off the bus. He hands me a quarter and I walk over to the payphone and page the dope man. He won't deliver to our side of the city. He stays in the neighborhoods where the majority of his customers are, so every day we drag our asses over the hill and use this payphone and wait. Most days we make the trip at least twice. It's as routine as shooting dope.

The phone rings, I pick it up, tell him it's me, and hang up.

"How long?" asks Saul.

"He said ten minutes."

"That would be a miracle."

I light a cigarette, and we walk down the block to wait.

TIME MANAGEMENT

SAN FRANCISCO, FEBRUARY 5, 1996

Come on, Pill Lady. I gotta go.

A patrol car turns the corner and slowly drives by. The cop, one hand on the steering wheel, removes his sunglasses and stares at me. It's the second time he's been around the block. First time I was standing here waiting and he saw me but didn't slow down. Now he's back to see what I'm doing. If he comes around again and I'm still here, he's going to stop. Then I'll have to deal with getting shoved against the car and searched, and him calling in to see if there's anything he can bust me for. I don't have the time for this shit right now. I hate coming to the Tenderloin, such a fucked-up neighborhood.

I lean down and rap twice with my knuckles on the top of the basement window, then turn slightly to look in the cop's direction. Behind me the metal gate to the hotel's entrance opens, a small woman dressed in a pink velour running suit pokes her head out and watches the patrol car as it drives away.

"What you want, baby?"

"Hey, Pill Lady," I say. "Got any Dolophine?"

"No, child." She glances up and down the street. "Got Dilaudids and Valiums."

"Fuck. That shit ain't got no legs," I say out loud to myself and then try to think who else is selling and will they give me credit. "I gotta work today," I tell her when I realize I'm fucked and no one else is going to help me out.

"You gotta job, baby?" she says and then looks up the street. "Honey, come inside before the poh-lees come back."

I grab the gate before it closes behind her. Although why I'm going inside, I don't know. She doesn't have what I want, and following her isn't going to make it appear. But the Pill Lady is the absolute best connection for prescription drugs, plus she gives me credit. She's at least seventy years old, maybe older, and only a couple inches over four feet tall. Always dressed in the latest ghetto-cool, she smokes crack like a fiend, shoots dope to come down, and never leaves her hotel room except to do business. She's a major player in this fucked-up neighborhood. Everybody knows her. All the pill scammers and fake script writers sell their shit to her wholesale. And then she turns around and sells it for twice her price to people like me that got no game.

Usually she has a steady flow of Dolophine, which is the pill form of Methadone, and better than that cherry-flavored liquid Metha-dose crap they dole out at the clinic. Although they don't get me high, a couple of Dolophines will keep me well for a few hours. Dilaudids are just synthetic morphine in a pill that you can crush and cook up like heroin, but it's a quick high, don't last long. So they're more of a luxury, or like now, something to do when there's nothing else.

An overflowing trashcan partially blocks the hotel's entrance and I step around it, make my way through the garbage and cigarette butts that litter the floor. The lobby reeks of mildew, cigarettes, and rotting greasy food. The walls, possibly painted white a long time ago, are now a dingy yellow and covered with graffiti. A single low-watt light bulb hangs from the ceiling, barely illuminating the hallway. A couple of signs proclaiming the hotel a drug-free zone and the management's right to refuse service to anyone hang crooked on a wall above a worn-out sofa so decrepit and stained that I've never seen anybody sit on it.

As we cross the lobby I glance toward the manager's office and see the door is closed, then look down at the Pill Lady. "Don't worry," she says. "Manager's not here."

There's a constant flow of drugs in this hotel, and the manager knows it. The bastard wants a piece of the action and charges me five bucks to go to the Pill Lady's room. That's why I knock on her window instead of just going inside.

Making our way down the stained and torn carpet, we walk toward the stairs to the basement at the end of the hall. An unconscious wino with dried puke on the front of his shirt sits propped up against the entrance to the stairwell, his outstretched legs blocking our way, an empty bottle lying on its side in a pool of liquid at his feet.

The Pill Lady pushes the bottle with her foot. "Could be beer, could be piss."

"Lemme give you a hand," I say and step over the drunk, offering the Pill Lady my arm. Gripping my elbow, she leans into me and together we walk down the stairs.

The basement is dark and in worse condition than the first floor: the stagnant air foul with the smell of shit and rotting garbage; the walls stained with layers of ancient grease and dirt. Sections of the hallway linoleum are missing and there's a dead rat in the corner, its head flattened in a trap. The first two rooms don't have doors. They're filled with torn mattresses, discarded chairs, and old pieces of unusable furniture. A fluorescent ceiling light flickers and blinks, giving off a strobe effect that leaves us stumbling in the dark every couple of seconds.

"Stay here a minute," says the Pill Lady as she opens the door to her room and then goes inside.

I glance back down the hall and scan the shadows as I touch the folded knife in my jacket pocket and lean against the wall by her door. A muffled thud echoes from somewhere above me. I hear a toilet flush as I light a cigarette, momentarily blinded by the lighter's flame.

"Got another smoke?" asks a man, his voice coming from somewhere behind me down at the end of the hall that's so dark I can't see anyone there.

"Nah, man. My last one."

"Wanna date, sugar?" This time it's a woman and she's a lot closer.

The door to the Pill Lady's room opens and she holds out her hand. In her palm are some blue pills and a few yellow ones.

"Dilaudids for five, and V's for a buck."

"Five for Dilaudids?" I say, wondering how I'm going to stay well all day. "Okay. One Dilaudid, five Valiums, and I'll owe you." I hand her a couple of dollars and head toward the stairs.

"Be careful, baby," she says and closes the door, the sound of her lock turning echoing in the dark hallway.

"Hey, sexy, come here for a second," says the woman standing in the doorway to one of the rooms filled with broken furniture. The ceiling light flickers on and I see her face. Her eyes are dull and vacant, her clothes torn and dirty. The hair on her head is flat and matted like she just got out of bed. Behind her a shadow moves and I turn and take the stairs two at a time.

At the front gate I slip one of the Valiums in my mouth, swallowing it with saliva, and put the rest in my pocket. Looking into the street, I hesitate, my hand on the latch, trying to see if I can spot the cop. The Valiums give me a buzz but don't do shit-all for my jones. But there isn't much I can do about it until I find a place I can shoot the Dilaudid and get well.

The sun is bright. The morning fog has lifted. It has to be around nine o'clock and I have to get across town. Last night a guy I know called and offered me a job painting a house and I said sure, be there at eight thirty. But that was last night right after I did a hit. I was high, everything looked like it was going to be all right. Then this morning the dope man said he didn't have any, told me to call back later. I told him I didn't have a later and he said there was nothing he could do and hung up. This job pays, but I have to be able to work. I can't be dope sick up on a ladder.

I walk toward Market Street, hoping I can get out of the neighborhood before that cop sees me. When I get to the intersection there's two patrol cars and a paddy wagon up the block and a group of cops standing around some dude spread against a wall, going through his pockets.

It must be sweep day. That's when every cop and parole officer in the city hits the streets busting parolees for not reporting. They shake down anyone suspicious, and if you don't have ID, or you're loaded, they stop you and run a warrant check. If you've got an unpaid ticket, an old warrant, you've absconded on your parole or probation, or they just don't like the way you look, than you're headed off to jail, no questions asked.

At the corner I slip into the liquor store and check out the scruffy old man at the counter, we both nod like we know each other. The store is a dump. Nothing but crap for sale: two-for-a-dollar packages of cookies, ramen noodles, canned pork and beans, and plenty of alcohol. The center aisle is crowded with porn magazines; lustrous full-lipped, half-naked women squeezing mammoth breasts together gaze out in some plausible imitation of sexual come-hither-ness. I stare at the glossy front covers all shrink-wrapped and protected from possible finger invasion and feel some sort of sexual tension as the implied possibilities seem more intriguing than the real thing.

At the rear of the store by the refrigerator section, a man stands looking at the beer with his back to me. Dressed in a soiled wife-beater and baggy black chinos, there's something about the way he's standing that's familiar, like my friend Sweet. I call his name, but he doesn't turn around, and I wonder if it's him, and then I remember Sweet is dead, that it couldn't be him.

I found Sweet in his bed. He'd been there for days and rigor mortis had set in. I smell the scent of his death and quickly take another Valium, then grab a Coke and walk back to the counter. I search my pockets for change and wait for the memory to fade, the intrusive smell to leave my nostrils.

"Semmi-five-sens," says the scruffy old man behind the counter, his accent so thick I have to concentrate to figure out what he's saying.

With less than a dollar fifty in my pocket, seventy-five cents is the difference between me walking or riding the bus. I leave the Coke on the counter and walk out as the old man yells in some language I don't understand.

Two crackheads hurry by, twitching and spastic in that universal crackhead gait. The one closest gives me the eye and says something, but it might as well be the language the scruffy old man was speaking because I can't understand him either.

"What the fuck you lookin' at?" I say and then turn around to check if any cops are close. Making a right, I head down the street and then take a left at the corner when I see the block is clear. Two more blocks and I'll be on Market Street, and then I can catch a streetcar.

A transvestite in a wedding dress steps out of a doorway and stumbles into me. I try to get out of the way but he grabs for me and I feel his hands grope my body.

"What the fuck," I yell, and push him away.

A tattered wig, full beard, and running mascara obscure his face as he tries to maintain his balance, but falls against the wall. He's so loaded he has to be on Ketamine or some of that GHB crap, or PCP, or some other drug not meant for human consumption. I watch as he crumples onto the sidewalk and passes out and wonder what the fuck he's doing wearing a wedding dress.

A group of people stand in the doorway of a hotel and watch the man in the wedding dress as he lies there comatose. Off to the side, holding a can of beer wrapped in a brown paper bag, is Freddy, a hope-to-die dope fiend I've known for years who has finally worked his way down the food chain to living in a piss-in-the-sink Tenderloin hotel.

"Not a good day for a walk," Freddy says.

"Tell me 'bout it," I say and step into the doorway. Two old guys dressed in matching button-down short-sleeve shirts and slacks who I assume work at the hotel move toward the transvestite. "What's up, man?" I ask Freddy, and we both watch as they turn the dude over and check to see if he's breathing.

"Same old shit," says Freddy. Although when I look at him I notice that life hasn't been good to him. He's lumpy and bloated and his skin is discolored. There's a runny sore on his lip and the whites of his eyes are yellow.

"You lookin'?" he asks and then takes a sip of beer.

"Was," I say. "You live here?"

"Yeah, if ya call this living," he says. "Need to get off the street?"

"Just for a minute, if ya know what I mean."

"Think I do," he says. "Come on."

Another dirty depressing hotel, another stained carpeted hallway, the omnipresent stench of rot, the universal air of decay. Although Freddy's hotel appears to be in a little better shape than the Pill Lady's, it's still just another decrepit place people find themselves in when they've nowhere else to go.

After walking up two flights of stairs, Freddy gestures to a door and opens it with a key. The room is cramped and dark and stinks of sweat and piss. A bare mattress on a metal frame sits in the center of the room. There's a small TV on a dresser by the window.

"Got any water?" I pull out my kit: a leather sunglass case containing a small teaspoon, a rig, and a ball of cotton.

Freddy points to a murky drinking glass on the dresser and I grab it. In the corner is a sink attached to the wall and I rinse the glass and fill it with fresh water. All the old hotel rooms in San Francisco have sinks like this. The main communal bathroom with a shower and toilet is down the hall. But in the middle of the night, if you have to go, you just take a leak in the sink. That's why they're called "piss-in-the-sink" hotels.

"What you got?" says Freddy.

"Dilaudid," I say as I crush the pill into my spoon.

"Possible I can get the cotton?"

"Not a problem," I mumble, the end of my belt in my mouth as I tie off and shoot the yellow liquid into my vein. What good the leftover residue from one Dilaudid will do Freddy is questionable at best, because I'm not leaving much in the spoon. However, it is customary junkie etiquette to kick down the cotton when that's all you've got and you're using someone else's room to shoot up in.

Handing over my spoon I watch Freddy squirt water onto the cotton and then press it with his grubby finger as he draws the nearly clear liquid into his syringe.

When he's done I take my spoon, put my kit away, and sneak a Valium into my mouth. I barely felt the Dilaudid, but hopefully it's enough to keep me well for the day.

"I gotta go," I tell Freddy ,who's sitting on the edge of the bed jabbing himself, trying to find a vein. Visions of a bloody sword fight come to mind as I slip out the door and head down the stairs to the hotel's entrance.

Outside there's an ambulance parked at the curb, the paramedics intent on lifting the unconscious transvestite onto a gurney. The two old men stand nearby smoking cigarettes and watching with unconcerned expressions. I cut around the ambulance, jaywalk across the street and duck into an alley. I feel better about the possibility of being stopped by the cops now that I don't have the Dilaudid on me, although I do have the rig and the burnt spoon and a couple of Valiums. So maybe it's just that the Valiums are starting to work their complacent magic.

I come to the end of the alley and walk quickly over to the next intersection, cross with the light and head down the hill into the Civic Center Plaza. It's a clear day and the sun is shining but all the benches usually filled with street people are empty and the park is deserted. A city worker sweeps up trash from the gutter as a meter maid putts along the edge of the park in her Cushman scooter. To my right is City Hall with its gleaming dome and flags snapping in the breeze. To my left is the new library where all the homeless people are hiding, waiting for sweep day to be over with.

I take the escalator down into the underground at Market Street and pay my fare before taking another flight of stairs to the station below. The job is out by City College, all the way across town. I check the overhead digital clock. Ten fifteen. It's getting late, and I'm at least an hour away.

I wait for the next streetcar and realize that I don't know which one takes me to City College. On the other side of the station there's a large map on the wall with color coordinated routes and I see I need to catch the K car and head back to the outbound platform to wait.

Its brakes screeching, a train pulls into the station. A woman walks by pushing a stroller, her child passed out and leaning to the side, its arm dragging on the dirty station floor. A man in an overcoat holding a newspaper stares at me and I stare back. I'm dying for a cigarette, but I only have a few left and need to make them last.

Another train approaches; it's not the car I want. A couple of gutter punks carrying skateboards walk up the platform laughing and shoving one another. One of them pulls out a large magic marker and quickly scribbles a cursive tag on the tile wall then stares in my direction as if I am going to say or do something. I look at him, dressed similar to me in torn black jeans and leather jacket, and wonder why he's crazy-eying me like that.

The station becomes quiet. No one talks. No trains come, and I feel the Valiums invading my brain. The dampness of being underground makes me shiver, but really I don't feel anything. It's more of an involuntary reaction. Staring at some advertisement for lite beer, I wonder why anyone would drink that shit and then laugh when I think about the possibilities of heroin lite and emaciated dope fiends worrying about their calorie intake.

Two more cars come and go with a thundering noise, and I ask a woman standing next to me what time it is and she tells me it's quarter of eleven. I reach into my jacket for cigarettes and see two transit cops walking down the platform and put the pack back in my pocket. The cops stop when they reach the gutter punks and one of them talks while the other stands off to the side, whispering into his radio. The punks shift around and look at the floor as they hand the cop their IDs. The woman next to me leans out over the platform and looks into the tunnel.

Another streetcar enters the station, blowing cool damp air in my face as it pulls to a stop. A family of tourists in shorts and T-shirts gets off, looking around as if they're lost. The father tells the two children to stick close to the mother and then he walks over to the transit cops and asks directions. The cop with the radio points upward and then goes back to the gutter punks. The father glances at the mother, who turns to the kids, and they all tromp past me to the stairs, a strange bewildered expression plastered across all their faces.

"What time is it?" I ask the woman standing next to me.

"Ten minutes later than the last time you asked," she says, and then moves away as the cops walk over and ask if I've got proof I paid my fare.

"What do you mean proof?"

"You have a transit pass or a transfer?" says the cop with the radio.

I feel around my pockets and can't seem to find one. I don't remember if I took a transfer at the fare booth or if I just walked on through. "Don't got one," I mumble, raise my shoulders in a shrug. The woman with the time steps farther away as the gutter punks walk up behind the cops.

The cop pulls out a black leather wallet and asks for my ID. "Going to have to write you a ticket."

"I paid my fare, dude." The words slur as they come out of my mouth and I can't think of anything else to say. Reluctantly, I hand over my ID.

The gutter punks start to yell at the cops. One of them says this is bullshit and that he saw me pay my fare. The other one, the graffiti artist, tells them this is harassment and to leave me alone. I look over at him and suddenly we're in solidarity when minutes ago he was acting like I was some sort of an authority figure.

The cop hands me the ticket. "Next time get a transfer."

I barely glance at it before jamming it in my pocket. The gutter punk tells the cops to fuck themselves as they walk away. The K pulls to a stop and I get on. The woman who I'd been asking for the time takes the seat across the aisle and tells me the ticket's expensive, a hundred-and-fifty-dollar fine.

"It doesn't matter," I say. "I'm not paying it anyway."

Leaning back in my seat, I close my eyes and rest my head against the window as the car rocks back and forth. My mouth is dry from the Valiums. I'm numb and want a cigarette. A hundred and fifty dollars is a lot of money and I start to get angry but realize it's fucking useless and drift off into the Valium high. The warmth feels so comfortable and I forget why I'm here and lean into the train as it pulls into a turn.

The streetcar is stopped with the motor running. The doors are open and there's nobody but me on board. I peer out the window and see we're above ground at a station. I sit up and rub my eyes. The operator walks up and tells me it's the end of the line: everybody has to exit the car.

I stumble onto the platform and light a cigarette. At first I have no idea where I am, then I see an exit sign for City College and start walking.

A group of kids run around screaming and I move over to avoid them as they barge through the station's gates. I think I'm a couple of blocks away from the job site, but I'm not sure, and I stop to ask a woman for directions. She stares at me as I talk, her expression is weird and I can't understand why she's looking at me the way that she is.

"Are you all right?" she says.

"I'm fine," I say and then drop my cigarette. Bending down to pick it up, I lose my balance and fall to one knee. Standing up, I fumble with the cigarette and finally get it into my mouth. "Just need directions," I mumble.

A cool breeze blows in from the ocean and I lean against a utility pole and feel the sun on my face. I want to lie down and take a nap. Off to the side of the station is a row of benches and I walk over and sit down. Pulling my jacket around me I close my eyes. Just need a few seconds, then I'll be on my way.

The scream of a siren wakes me up. Startled, I watch an ambulance weave its way through the congested traffic on the street in front of me.

I'm sitting on a bench and there is no one else anywhere near me.

I fumble in my pocket for my pack of cigarettes and pull out a crumpled ticket. I really don't remember what it is and I'm surprised to see that my name on it. I'm dehydrated, my mouth tastes like shit. I'm tired and my body is stiff. I wonder what time it is and then remember I'm supposed to be at a job. Then I remember the Pill Lady, Freddy, and getting the ticket. I start feeling anxious and look around to see where I am. The buildings of City College are off to my right and I begin walking. A few blocks in front of me there's a large sign for Beep's Burgers, a drive-in I was told the job was close to.

At the corner I can see a house with a guy up on a ladder and drop cloths covering the ground. As I get closer I notice another guy scraping old paint off the window molding and the dude who called me about the job standing on the sidewalk in front of the building staring at me.

"Hey," I say as I walk up.

"Hey what?" says the dude.

"Sorry I'm a little late," I say and unzip my jacket.

"A little late?" he says. "It's two in the afternoon, man."

"I had trouble gettin here," I say and reach into my pocket and pull out the ticket. "The fuckin' transit cops stopped me, wrote me a ticket. I paid the fare, man. I wasn't doin' nothin' wrong."

The dude just stands there, stares at me. I try to think of something else to say, to think of another reason why I'm so late, but I can't think of anything, and instead look down at the ground to avoid his gaze.

"What do you want me to start on?" I ask as I shove the ticket in my pocket and take off my jacket.

He gestures to the man up on the ladder. "I already called another guy."

"Fuck, dude," I say. "Ain't my fault. I was trying to get here."

"I told you last night the job started at eight thirty." He leans into my face. "I need people I can depend on, man. I got a schedule to keep."

"Dude, I need this job. I need money."

"Then you shoulda been here on time." He turns to the guy scraping the windows. "Hey, man, make sure you caulk those before you put the primer on, okay?"

"Can't I work the rest of the day?"

"We quit at four, man. What the fuck?" he says, walking away.

"You know it cost me time and effort to get here," I say as I follow him.

"What?"

"Can you at least kick me down some cash? I came all the way out here. And I got a fuckin' ticket, man."

"You don't show up, I have to get another worker, the day's almost done, and you come here loaded and want me to pay you money."

"I got a fuckin' ticket," I scream.

He turns toward the building. "Get the fuck outta here."

"Thanks, man. Thanks a lot. I'll fuckin' never work for you again."

"You ain't worked for me yet," he says, then leers at the guy on the ladder and they both laugh.

When I get to the train station I sit back down on the bench and light a cigarette. I don't have enough money for the fare to get back. I was counting on getting paid for working today. Now all I have is a couple Valiums and Jenny waiting for me at home expecting me to have money for dope.

I can't believe how fucked up this is. A fucking ticket. Those guys back there laughing at me. *I tried to get here. I am here, damn it. Should've let me work, that asshole. Should've at least paid me for my time. Could've just stayed home, man. Fuckin' can't believe how unfair this is. Why does this shit always happen to me?*

I stand up and walk toward the station, scanning the ground for a transfer someone might have dropped. A couple of kids that look like they go to City College walk toward me and I ask if they've got any spare change because I need to get on the streetcar. One of them hands me his transfer and I walk into the station.

THE GUN

"What do I want with a gun?" I say.

"It's worth a couple hundred." The twitchy speed freak is going by the name of Dave. Last month he was Andrew. Next time I see him, who knows? He changes his name depending on how bad his paranoia is, in the hopes it will keep the pursuers, imaginary or otherwise, off his tail. I wonder if he has as much trouble remembering his name as I do.

"Yeah, but, ah, Dave. I need money. Not a gun."

"Everyone needs a gun," says Dave, although why he doesn't need one as well sort of shoots holes through that theory.

I try to avoid speed freaks—their nervous energy fucks up my high. There I am ready to nod out in opiated euphoria and they're yapping away a mile a minute about fuck-all while jerking around like an epileptic in a fit. And forget about having them over to the house. Their happy fingers dance through your stuff like a klepto at Kmart.

However, tonight's encounter with Dave isn't a social call. Having recently come into some cash, Jenny and I had entered into the speed-dealing business so we could make some money to pay for our habits. Only it wasn't our cash—it was Jenny's mother's money.

●

Ever since Jenny was a little girl, her mother had been depositing money in a bank account for her college fund. Because the account was in both their names, Jenny had access. During one of their usual terse phone conversations her mom slipped and inadvertently mentioned the account. Jenny made some inquires, found out it was true, and then promptly withdrew a few thousand dollars.

We'd struck gold—a dope fiend's dream come true. Before we'd even spent the money we went back to the bank for more. But this time a stern-looking manager pulled us aside and asked if he could speak with Jenny privately. Sequestered in an office cubical, he told her she was no longer on the account and asked her to leave. Jenny's eyes went all wide. She stood up and walked out into the middle of the lobby and started yelling it was her money and to quit fucking with her. The manager cringed, customers stared, but we didn't get any more cash. Her mother, having been alerted, had somehow figured a way to stop Jenny from making any more withdrawals.

With a little over a thousand dollars left, we decided we needed to find a way to make money. That's when I proposed the idea of buying speed. Because, I told Jenny, we didn't do speed, and if we bought some to sell we'd make a profit we could use to buy heroin. The only problem was having to deal with nervous twitching speed freaks like Dave coming over to our apartment at all hours of the night.

"Can't do it," I say. "I need cash."

"Come on," he pleads. "Two grams. That's like giving it to you."

"No way."

"Okay, one gram," he says and hands me the gun.

I don't even want to hold it, but for some reason I take it from him. It's a large .38 revolver that feels heavy in my hands. It isn't sexy. It isn't sleek. It's just an ugly thug of a gun. Pushing the release I slip open the cylinder, relieved to see there aren't any bullets inside.

"I'll give you half a gram for this fuckin' thing," I say. "I don't want it. But it's kind of cool. Maybe I can sell it to somebody."

"All right!" he says, a little too quickly, and I wonder if this thing even works.

I hand him a tiny Ziploc with four small yellow lumps inside.

"Can I use your bathroom?"

"No fuckin' way, man. Go somewhere else to shoot up."

The room is dark. The lights are off. My nose is running and my head aches. The muscles in the back of my legs cramp and twitch. My gut feels as if it's about to explode. I'm covered in sweat. I'm rocking back and forth naked. I want a cigarette, but the idea of sucking in smoke makes me retch. I run my fingers through my damp hair and realize I have to get out of bed and pull at the clammy sheets. I'm trying not to disturb Jenny as she tosses and turns in her own hell. I stand up and I'm immediately freezing. I start shaking. I want to puke, and I don't know if I can get to the bathroom.

I shuffle across the trash-covered floor of the living room and push open the door. Grabbing the sink for support I lower myself onto the toilet. Slimy liquid shit pours out of me before I can sit down. I wrap my arms around my sides while every muscle in my body aches. Bile rises in my throat and I turn, spraying the wall.

"Fuck," I try to yell, but it's little more than a hiss. I look for toilet paper but there is none. I'm shivering as I pick a dirty towel up off the floor and wrap it around me. Dim light from the window illuminates the bathtub, its mildewed shower curtain hangs limp from a bar along the ceiling. *What time is it? What day is it?*

I wipe myself with the towel and toss it on the floor and stumble out of the bathroom. The living room is dark, all the curtains are drawn, the stagnant air smells of cigarettes and something rotten. Midway across the room my vision blurs, and I feel dizzy. I stop and lean on a chair, and wait for it to pass. In front of me, lying on the desk, is the gun. Maybe I could pawn it? But you can't trust a speed freak. Who knows where it's been? If it's hot, it could be traced back to me. Wouldn't that be perfect? Busted for somebody else's shit.

Dealing speed hadn't worked out like I'd planned. Although we had sold most of it, we hadn't sold it quick enough, and we weren't able to re-up to keep selling, and we ended up spending all the money. Now we had nothing, were stuck in the limbo of kicking. Lying around, waiting for something, anything.

As I crawl back into bed, Jenny looks up. Her black hair, matted and damp against her olive skin, frames her face. Dark circles have formed under her eyes.

"This sucks," she sighs.

"I know." I reach for a cigarette. "You want a smoke?"

"No," she says, sitting up. "What are we gonna do?"

"We're doing it."

"This sucks," she says.

"I know."

A phone rings far away, somewhere in a dream. I don't want to wake up. I'd rather sleep. I must have passed out.

"Hello?" I cautiously answer. Anyone could be on the other end: people I owe money to or have ripped off, family members wondering where we've been, the landlord looking for rent.

"Hey," says Nolan.

"Hey, man. What's up?" I answer, knowing that if Nolan is calling he's looking for dope.

"Can you score me some?"

"Yeah," I say. "But we're sick. Haven't had any in days. Can you throw some our way? Or least lend me some money so we can get well?"

"Man, I'll do you right. Don't worry," he says. "Saul's with me, okay?"

"No problem." I hang up the phone. "Jenny, it's gonna be all right."

"What's with the gun?" Saul is checking out the .38 on my desk. We're sitting around after having gotten high. Nolan gave Jenny and me a quarter gram to split. Just barely enough to get us well— the last two days of hell forgotten.

"Why? You want to buy it?" I say.

"What do I want with a gun?"

"I don't know. You could knock off liquor stores or something."

"Yeah, I guess I could," Saul says, and we laugh.

Saul and Nolan are about as close to friends as I have, though all we really have in common is heroin. A couple years earlier Nolan had been a pretty successful dealer and I used to buy from him. Then some scumbags ripped him off. A month later he got busted. Out on bail, he's currently fighting a sales case.

I can't remember when, but Nolan introduced me to Saul, who is a little more together than Nolan and sure as hell easier to get along with. Saul was one of those guys that when you met him for the first time it felt as if you already knew him. Saul stays with us off and on when he doesn't have a place of his own. Lately we've been hanging out together. Pooling our money to buy larger quantities of drugs.

"What's going on?" asks Nolan.

"Nothing goin' on," I tell him. "We're broke."

"Thought you were dealing?"

"Sold it all," I say. "Money's gone."

"What are you gonna do?" asks Saul.

"Don't know, man. I really don't know."

Technically, kicking heroin takes three days. Every junkie's kick is slightly different, yet the symptoms are the same. For me it starts out with an unpleasant familiar taste in the back of my throat. My nose begins to run, I sneeze a lot, and my eyes water. Then the aches arrive, followed by vomiting and diarrhea. There's no sleeping. I'm either cold and shivering or hot and continually sweating. My muscles cramp, my head feels thick, and all I think about is doing more dope in order to not be in such misery.

Physically, it's all about endorphins, a morphine-like substance naturally produced by the pituitary gland as a way of dealing with all the normal aches and pains that humans experience on a daily basis. Exercise and sex, as well as other pleasurable activities, cause it to be released. When external opiates, such as heroin, are introduced in massive junkie-like quantities, the body stops producing endorphins. Withdrawal is simply the body catching up, downtime between shooting up and the natural process of the central nervous system picking up the slack.

The first time I kicked it felt like a cold, and I really didn't know what it was until another dope fiend with years more experience clued me in. The next time it was a lot worse, as I knew what to expect. As my tolerance increased and I needed more dope in order to maintain the same high, or as is usually the case just to stay well, the kick got unbearable, the symptoms more exaggerated. At this point the thought is enough for me to do anything in order to avoid it all.

"I can't take it," I say to Jenny, who's so intent on watching television she barely hears me. A mass of unruly black hair covers the side of her face, hangs down over her skinny body, a thin shoulder protruding. "There's never enough. We're always sick. I'm fuckin' goin' nuts."

"Huh?" says Jenny.

"Fuck," I yell, spastically knocking over the ashtray, sending butts and ashes everywhere.

"Jesus, babe. You okay?"

In the last two weeks we hadn't been able to put together one solid day of staying high. Either we were sick lying in bed waiting for someone to call looking for drugs, or scraping together twenty dollars for a quarter gram, which only kept us well for a few hours. Then we'd be sick again—another sleepless night of agony, another day lying in bed waiting for the phone to ring.

I'd shoplifted from every store in the neighborhood, stealing batteries, razor blades, and electric toothbrushes I could sell to those shady characters that hung around the all-night donut shop in the Mission. But after months of strolling through the local businesses never buying anything and always ducking out with bulging pockets and backpacks, the stores had wised up and now there were security guards and electronic sensors that set off alarms when shit left the store the wrong way.

Then I'd found a box of checks from an account I had closed years ago. For a short time I passed worthless checks to every store that would take them. That had played out quick, and now some of those stores, angry about being stiffed, weren't allowing me inside.

As a last resort I had even walked around the neighborhood begging for money with a gas can, telling everyone my car had just run out of gas. Which had worked the first few times, but once the locals were familiar with the scam they steered clear of me. A junkie with no hustle is a sad sight indeed.

It's freezing in the apartment, but I can't stay in bed. The idea of spending another night sprawled out sweating, shaking, puking, and shitting is fucking crazy. I can't look at Jenny lying there next to me, her eyes pleading, her body withering and twitching in pain.

The digital clock on the desk in the living room reads 11:53 PM. I light a cigarette and stare at the gun. Before I can really think about it, I pull on a pair of jeans and get dressed. Digging through a pile of dirty clothes, I find a black bandana and tie it loosely around my neck. I slip the gun into my waistband, button my overcoat, and quickly open the front door.

The streets are deserted, the traffic light. Three blocks away there's a commercial strip of stores, restaurants, banks, and bars. The other night, when I went for cigarettes, there'd been a line of people at the ATM.

Cautiously I cross the street, making my way toward the bank. Off to the side of the ATM are some bushes and shadows to hide in. I crouch and slip the bandana over my face.

Hearing someone approach I step into the light. A guy about my age, dressed in a suit, stares at me. His mouth open, debit card in hand. I point the gun. Tell him to take out as much money as he can. Hesitating, he stands stiff, staring at the gun and I notice I'm shaking so bad the barrel is practically bouncing up and down.

The sound of people loudly talking over music from the bar across the street floats on the air. Dense slabs of fog break through the trees above me. A taxi slows down looking for fares. Under the bank's overhead lights I feel like I'm on display. Unsure of what to do next I take off running, the gun still in my hand. When I turn the corner I think I hear shouting, and I break into a sprint. Breathing hard, my lungs feel like they're about to give out.

Down the block a couple gets out of a car and enters an apartment building. I catch the front door before it closes. They turn around as I rush inside, the bandana still covering my face.

"Oh my god," screams the woman.

"Your money," I gasp, and point the gun at them.

"We don—we don't want no trouble," the man stammers, scrambling for the wallet in his back pocket.

"Here, take it," hisses the woman, her face an expression of terror as she shoves a shiny black leather purse in my direction.

I back out of the lobby clutching the purse and wallet, then turn and run. I'm only a block and a half from my apartment, but I'm not sure I can run anymore. Pushing myself, I will my legs to make those last few steps before ducking into my building's entrance.

Inside, the apartment feels confining, yet its familiar darkness and damp smell is comforting. Pouring out the contents of the purse I see a couple of fives, a ten, and some change. Opening the wallet I shakily count five crisp twenty-dollar bills. I'm scared. I'm having trouble breathing. I think I'm going to puke.

Jenny's eyes flash to the small pile of bills on the bed. "Where'd you get the money?"

"Never mind," I say as I pull on my boots, readying to leave.

I'd spent another sleepless night replaying the robberies over and over in my mind: the bewildered guy at the ATM, the frightened woman with the purse, the unloaded gun in my hand shaking like crazy.

The adrenaline rush of the night's events had somehow kept me from being totally dope sick. An hour ago I'd woken Jenny and we'd had sex, something we hadn't done for a long time. Being strung out pretty much destroys my sex drive. The surprise on her face when I gripped her ass with both my hands and came reminded me of how long it had actually been since we even tried.

Holding her in my arms I told her I loved her. She kissed me, told me she loved me too. That's when I said I had a surprise and showed her the money.

"Where'd you get the money?"

"There are some things it's better you don't know about," I say.

"Fuck you." Jenny pulls the covers off, exposing dark nipples. "When ya get back from scoring, you're gonna tell me."

"I robbed some people last night," I say. "I came up on them. Stuck the gun in their faces and took their shit."

"Fuck, babe." Jenny stares at me with her mouth open—full lips surrounding perfect white teeth. Jenny could be a model with the looks she has: Italian, olive skin, dark complexion. At twenty years old she could have been a lot of things besides a junkie.

"Problem is, they're neighbors. Hope they don't recognize me if I run into them."

"Fuck, babe," she says again.

The cigarette smoldering between my fingers wakes me as it melts into my skin and I shake it free from my hand. "Mutha fuck," I mumble and try to lick the burn but my lips are dry, and my throat feels made of cardboard. I grab a Coke that's sitting by the bed. The liquid is warm and sweet, there's hardly any carbonation.

Jenny lies next to me facing the TV, her feet resting on pillows by my head. In front of her are three small rolled-up balloons full of dope. Lined up like she's playing with marbles, each one a different color. I look at the clock; it's three in the afternoon. There's some stupid woman screaming on the television. I hear a phone ringing, but it's faint, and I can't tell where it's coming from.

"Can you get the phone?" I ask.

"What?" Jenny stares at the pointless sitcom, the laugh track a faint murmur.

"The phone. Answer the fuckin' phone."

"You answer the fuckin' phone. It's closer to you."

"Where is it?"

"Under the pillows," she says, lifting her feet.

Pushing aside the blankets and pillows I grab the phone.

Saul's voice comes through the distorted static of a bad connection. "What are ya doin'?"

"What do you mean, what am I doin'?"

A clear liquid weeps from the burn between my fingers. Pulling the phone cord free from under the covers, I light another cigarette, cradle the receiver to my ear with my shoulder, flinch as I dab the wound with a corner of the blanket.

"Still got that gun?" says Saul.

"Yeah, why?"

"Babe?" says Jenny.

"Hold on, Saul." I move the phone from my ear. "Yeah, Jenny, what do you want?"

"Why they wrap dope in balloons?" She's holding a pink one above her head, as if I needed to see an example.

"So you can swallow them," I answer.

"Hey, you there?" asks Saul.

"Yeah, I'm here."

"I got an idea," says Saul.

"Swallow them?" says Jenny.

"Hold on, Saul," I say. "Babe, they put the dope inside the balloon. They tie it tight. Then roll it inside itself. Cop pulls you over? You swallow it. Dope's protected. Won't dissolve in your stomach. You can shit it out, unwrap it, still good to shoot."

"Eeewww," says Jenny.

"Hey," says Saul, "you done with the shitting out dope lesson?"

"Yeah," I say. "What do ya want?"

"They look like fuckin' Easter eggs," says Jenny.

"I have an idea," says Saul.

"Like selling the gun?" I ask.

"Nah, more like using the gun," he says.

"Really?"

"We got heroin Easter eggs," says Jenny.

"Think we could make some money," says Saul.

"Malted milk balls with dope inside," says Jenny.

"I know we could make some money," I say.

"Want I come over, we talk about it?" asks Saul.

"Yeah, come over."

"Who's comin' over?" asks Jenny.

"Saul," I say.

"Can he pick up some candy?"

"Saul? Can you…"

"I heard," says Saul.

"Will you?"

"Yeah," says Saul. "You know she wants a cat."

"A what?" I say.

"Told me she wants a cat."

"Peanut butter cups and Skittles," says Jenny.

"No fuckin' way," I say.

"I can't have peanut butter cups and Skittles?"

"I'm talkin' to Saul."

"She says you love cats," says Saul.

"I fuckin' hate 'em."

"Aw, Patrick. We all know you're just a big softy that loves furry little animals and crazy girls half his age."

"Fuck you, Saul."

"Tropical Skittles," says Jenny.

"Got any dope?" asks Saul.

"Nah," I say, "we're out. You?"

"Got a little," says Saul. "Kick you down when I get there."

"Don't forget the Skittles."

"Tropical Skittles," says Jenny.

"And kitty litter?"

"Fuck you, Saul."

"And peanut butter cups," yells Jenny.

I'm Starving

In the refrigerator are five cakes: carrot, lemon, raspberry swirl, three-layer chocolate, and some kind of tiramisu, or maybe it's mocha. I can't tell. Five large, heavily frosted cakes, a slice or two missing from each. Otherwise, the refrigerator is empty. I want a cheeseburger. I want fries. I want anything but cake.

Two days ago Saul and I robbed a local bakery. Saul took the cakes too. Hungry, I stand in front of the refrigerator with the door open. At my feet is a cat. I stare at the cat. It stares at me. I look at the cakes. So does the cat. I look back at the cat. It looks up at me.

"Hey, whose fuckin' cat is this?" I ask. The kitchen window is open. I push the cat toward it with my foot. The cat looks at me, looks at the cakes, and walks toward the window, its tail sticking straight up in the air.

"It's a fuckin' zoo," I say. "It's a fuckin' cat zoo with cakes."

"Who are you talking to?" Jenny's in the bedroom, in bed. We've done our morning shots. I'm in that space where I know I have to figure out what I'm doing today. I have to eat. I have to get Jenny to eat. I have to do a robbery. I have to score more drugs. I have to buy cigarettes. I have to put some clothes on. I'm standing in front of the refrigerator, naked.

"There's some strange cat in here."

"A Siamese?"

"Yeah."

"That's our cat."

I push my finger into the thick white icing on the carrot cake, scrape off an inch and stick it in my mouth. The combination of butter, cream cheese, and sugar explodes on my tongue and I almost gag. I close the refrigerator, pick a half-smoked cigarette from the ashtray, lean down, and light it off the stove.

"We got a fuckin' cat?"

Saul is in the bathroom standing in front of the mirrored medicine cabinet. He's applying theatrical glue to his face. With a practiced movement, he presses the fake beard and mustache to his upper lip and chin. He turns, sees me watching standing in the doorway. He looks like some demented lumberjack-junkie, except he's dressed in a three-piece suit. I'm dressed in slacks and a button-down shirt. I can't find my shoes.

"Jenny, you seen my shoes?"

She doesn't answer. She's probably asleep. Jenny can sleep. Like all day long. I dig through a pile of dirty clothes, find a wrinkled tie and put it on. The toe of one of my shoes sticks out from under a chair. I reach down, grab it, see the other one, and pull it toward me.

Saul is waiting by the door, attaché case in hand. I pick up my suit jacket and we walk out into the alleyway that leads to the front of the building.

"You got the piece?" I ask. Saul pats the inside breast pocket of his suit and smiles. I light a cigarette as we walk toward the supermarket two blocks away. It's a beautiful afternoon. The sun is shining, the sky is clear. My mouth tastes like shit. I forgot to brush my teeth.

"Is my breath bad?" I say and lean toward Saul and blow at him.

"Don't breathe on me," says Saul. His newly acquired facial hair looks really fake in the sunlight.

In the supermarket parking lot I spot what we need: it's an older Honda Civic that looks to be in good shape. I slip the slim jim's hooked end down between the window and the door's rubber seal and jiggle it until it catches, then abruptly pull it upward. The door's lock mechanism clicks. I open the door and get in.

I take a screwdriver and wire cutters from my suit pocket and force the plastic housing off the steering column and then jam the end of the screwdriver into the ignition. Prying the entire lock off I expose the three contact points attached to the wires: power, ignition, and starter. With the cutters I snip the wires, then strip the ends and twist the power and ignition together, and touch the starter lead, which sparks as I press the gas pedal. The engine hesitates then roars to life and I feel smugly satisfied at having picked the right car.

I lean over and unlock the passenger door and Saul gets in. I hit the gas and pull out of the parking lot as I light another cigarette and adjust the rearview mirror. I look at Saul. He looks tense. The bank is only five minutes away.

"Why do I have to go in alone?" says Saul.

"We've been over this," I say. Saul can't drive. He never learned how. "Can't leave a stolen car running at the curb. It just doesn't look right. It says, hey, there's a fuckin' robbery going on. I know how to drive. I stay with the car."

"I hate going in alone."

It is always better to have two people for a bank job. It can get a little crazy inside. We've looked around, but everyone we know who dabbles in this sort of activity is either too high, too sketchy, or just way too insane. The last thing we need is someone's nerve getting the better of them. Then there we are coming out of the bank and the car is gone. Not my idea of a getaway.

Turning onto Union Street I drive past the bank. There's no one out front, and the pedestrian traffic on the sidewalk is relatively sparse. A mailman with a large leather bag slung over his shoulder chats with a woman standing in the doorway of a high-end boutique.

"Drive 'round the block," Saul says. A precaution we always take. Never know if a cop is eating at a local restaurant, or some meter maid with a police radio is close by handing out parking tickets.

The neighborhood is quiet. Everything seems normal. I pull up to the bank's front door and double-park. Saul sighs, gets out, and walks into the bank. I adjust my tie in the rearview mirror. Traffic is light. There are no cars behind me. I look over at the bank, but can't see in the window, the sun's reflection is too bright. Down the block an oncoming car stops and backs into a parking space. I look in the rearview mirror. I look over at the sidewalk. I glance at the bank. Sweat runs down my face. A city bus passes. A woman pushing a stroller stops in front of a store and then continues walking. I look at the gas gauge. The tank is half full. I want a cigarette, but I don't want to lose my concentration. I check the rearview mirror. See my reflection. I glance at the bank. I look across the street. A woman gets out of her car, walks around to the parking meter. I check the rearview mirror again. I wipe my forehead with my hand and run my fingers through my hair. Then I reach over and open the passenger door. I look over my shoulder. I look at the bank. I release the parking brake. I grip the steering wheel and look over as Saul comes out and walks to the car.

Before he's all the way inside I push down hard on the gas pedal and we take off, tires squealing. My heart pounds as the car accelerates. At high speed I make the intersection, swerve around the corner, drive two blocks, and turn again. Sliding through the next intersection, I ignore the stop sign, slip in between a taxi and a delivery van, then make a quick left and drive down a deserted alley.

Saul opens the attaché case; inside are two stacks of twenties, a few loose hundreds, tens, and fives. It's an okay haul. You never get as much as what you're expecting. Thumbing through a wad of money Saul stops when he feels a strange piece of plastic.

"Look at this," he says and holds up a clear circuit board with metallic copper strips and a small round battery glued to the back of a twenty.

"Tracer?" I say.

"Who the fuck knows? It sure as hell ain't money," he says and hands it to me with a couple of loose bills—getaway money once I ditch the car.

Two blocks before my apartment building, I slow down. At the corner I pull to the curb and Saul gets out, casually adjusts his suit, and walks away, briefcase in hand. I push down hard on the gas, drive to the end of Fillmore Street and maneuver the car into the commuter traffic on Marina Boulevard. Five minutes later I make a right at the entrance to the yacht club and slip into the first open spot in their parking lot. Picking up my tools I place them in my coat pocket and get out, kicking the door closed with my foot.

The Golden Gate Bridge rises in front of me out of the Bay, the water glistening in the afternoon sun—a nice view any other time. I walk past the sailboats moored at the dock, stop at a trashcan and toss in the weird circuit board. At a concession stand I buy a pack of cigarettes, take one out, light it, and walk along the breakwater toward home.

Bank jobs are a motherfucker. Even when I'm driving my adrenaline's pumped so high I'm jacked up for hours afterward. Going inside is even worse. Your senses are so hyped up. There's all these people staring at you, scared as hell—you definitely have to have your intimidating demeanor down to a science to be in control. It's all in the acting, baby.

The minute you pull the gun you have ninety seconds to finish the job and get out, as ninety seconds is the minimum possible amount of time it takes the police to respond to a bank's silent alarm. If you're alone, you stand in line waiting your turn and when you get to the teller you show the gun. You have to be discreet. You have to act quickly. You have to get in and get out before somebody realizes what's going on and triggers the alarm.

Below the counter is the working cash drawer, which holds a few thousand dollars and is the quickest to access. The other, the large drawer, holds more, but takes an additional key to open, which takes more time. Unless you're doing a takeover job where one gunman holds everyone at bay while another empties the drawers, your best chance is the working drawer and whatever money is inside.

Then there are the disguises: glasses, fake beards, mustaches, even fake ponytails hanging out the back of baseball caps. Cheap suits, athletic gear, army fatigues, and security guard uniforms can be worn over regular clothing and then tossed—anything to confuse witnesses. We once went in wearing motorcycle helmets and riding gear then fled the scene in a van, certain the cops were on the lookout for anyone on a bike that fit our description. Stolen cars, taxicabs, and bicycles all come in handy for getting away. Although I've simply just walked off, blending into the crowd.

When I cross Marina Boulevard I see the dope man's cheesy Mustang in the driveway of my apartment building. Jenny must have called him the minute Saul walked in the door. Since we've been buying larger quantities he's been more than willing to deliver.

My stomach growls. I feel lightheaded and I still haven't eaten. A warm breeze ruffles the hedges alongside a pink stucco building. Somewhere a bird sings, a sleek new Mercedes drives by, and I realize I'm walking past my mother's house. Which shouldn't surprise me, we practically live next door.

I glance up, half expecting to see her staring down at me. If she were she'd sure as hell be wondering what I was doing wearing a suit. Just last week she told me I was a fraud. I thought she was insinuating I was lying about being strung out, so I asked her what she meant.

"You dress like you grew up in the ghetto."

"Mom, people in ghettos don't dress like me."

"Your clothes are old and frayed and your jeans have holes in them," she continued. "You dress like you're trying to look poor. You're a fraud."

"Not like I gotta buncha money to spend on clothes."

"You dress like a thug."

"Mom!" I yelled. "Been wearing the same fuckin' clothing for years. Now all of sudden ya wanna call me a fraud."

"It's not just the clothes. You don't take care of yourself. You don't bathe. You smell up my house."

Unfortunately this was true. I almost never showered. I hated the feel of water on my skin. When I washed my hair it lay flat.

I preferred it dirty, sticking out in all directions. Apparently the universal junkie look wasn't what my mother wanted for her son. Hardly a wholesome image—mine having mutated from punk to dope fiend: black T-shirts, motorcycle boots, and torn Levi's. Of course, the money I had never went to buying clothes. Although, occasionally, when shopping at thrift stores for disguises, I'd also buy a pair of jeans or another T-shirt—but the only reason I bought them was because they looked like all the rest of the clothes I wore.

"Maybe, if you took better care of yourself, you wouldn't be so depressed and somebody would offer you a job," she said.

Those final words of hers reverberate in my mind as I smile and push open my apartment building's entrance. It's a beautiful afternoon, there's dope waiting for me, and we've enough money for the next couple days. At least tonight we'll be high and eating something besides cake.

"Hey, baby," Jenny coos as I walk through the door. She's on the futon in the bedroom, four balloons of dope by her side. I pass by Saul sitting in the living room smoking heroin off tin foil. The pungent sweet smoke envelops me and I want to puke.

"Hey," I say to Jenny and sit down, pushing aside her messy hair, disheveled from lying in bed all day. I touch her face, her dark eyes light up as she smiles. Holding her chin I kiss her, then reach for the drugs.

The dope is strong. My eyes barely open as I pull the rig out of my arm. I scratch the bridge of my nose and fumble with the cigarettes, but I can't seem to get hold of one. Dropping the pack I lie back and feel warm dullness through my entire body. I remember thinking something about my mother, but can't remember what it was. I stare at the television. A masked boogeyman runs a butcher knife across a woman's throat, the sound turned so low her screams are far away. The cat jumps up, walks across the bed, and stands on my chest. Its paws feel like steel rods pressing into me, its face inches from mine.

"Whose fuckin' cat is this?" I ask and then pet it on the head and scratch behind its ears—the purring becoming louder as I close my eyes.

THE PRICE OF FAME

San Francisco Marina Times
Criminal Gang Targeting the Marina District

Two well-armed and highly organized criminals have been terrorizing the neighborhoods of Chestnut Street, Cow Hollow, Union Street and Pacific Heights, targeting numerous shops, restaurants, and banks.

Thursday night, two men, whom the police have dubbed the Men in Black for their habit of dressing entirely in black, robbed Bella Pizzeria. Owner Vince Spagotti said the men entered his restaurant through a back door during business hours and robbed an employee at gunpoint. "They robbed the place without anyone knowing. Held the gun on my counterman while the restaurant was full of customers."

Police suspect the men are the same pair responsible for the recent string of brazen armed robberies that have plagued the Chestnut Street shopping district. San Francisco Police Detective John O'Leary said the police welcome any information the public may be able to provide. "We'll catch them," said O'Leary, "it's just a matter of time."

The pair are described as two males, age unknown, slight to medium build, ruddy complexion, possibly Hispanic. Any information, please contact the San Francisco Police Department.

"Check it out, man. We're fuckin' famous."

Saul comes out of a nod on the living room couch. "Say what?"

"We made the front page, dude."

"Lemme see." Saul scratches his nose as he holds the newspaper inches from his face trying to focus. "Men in black?"

"I know. Better start wearing some other color."

"Hispanic?"

"Obviously they're talkin' bout you," I say.

"I ain't Hispanic."

"Well I sure as hell ain't Hispanic."

"How the fuck can anyone say what we are? All they see is two eyes, an inch of forehead and a couple of eyebrows showin' through a ski mask."

"Fuckin' racism, man," I say. "You should write a letter to the editor. Tell 'em you're white and pissed off some Mexican gangster is getting credit for your shit."

"Fuck you."

"Here, let me see that," I say, taking the paper into the kitchen. I grab a pair of scissors and cut out the article. "Babe, we got any tape?"

"Wha'?" Jenny says. Lying in bed, comatose as usual with the TV on. "Any more Hostess cupcakes?"

"Jenny. Scotch tape. We got?"

"I don't know."

"Fuck."

"I don't use tape," she says. "Did you eat all the cupcakes?"

On the floor is a sticker from some forgotten punk band. Peeling off the backing, I rip it in half and use the pieces to attach the article to the kitchen wall.

Saul runs his hand over it. "Nice."

"It'll be like our scrapbook."

"I'm hungry," says Saul.

"What you wanna eat?"

"Don't know."

"Jenny, you wanna eat?"

"Jack in the Box."

"Breakfast Jack, no meat?"

"Yeah," she says.

"That'll work," says Saul. "Jack's is like the only place in the neighborhood we haven't robbed."

It's Saturday morning and Chestnut Street is full of yuppies flowing onto the sidewalk out of the bagel and coffee shops. Dressed in sweats and clutching their to-go coffees, every one of them looks so goddamn healthy. Not a hair out of place: white perfect teeth, designer sunglasses, unscuffed tennis shoes.

"Ever feel like you don't belong?" asks Saul.

"Actually, I think the question is, do you ever feel like you do belong."

"Too true, my man. Too true."

"Can I take your order, sir?" asks the woman behind the counter. Looking uncomfortable dressed in her uniform, she keeps pulling at the collar trying to adjust something. Yet the way she stares at me with her eyes slightly closed, or maybe it's the way her tongue slips across her lips when she talks, reminds me of someone, but I'm not sure who.

Behind her is a glowing sign for a new soft drink. Up by the ceiling are pictures of various combination meals: burgers with fries and a drink, chicken bits with onion rings, tacos, breakfast deals, desserts. The choices are overwhelming and I just stand there staring, wondering if I know her.

"Sir," she says, somewhat annoyed. "May I help you?"

"Yes, when I make up my mind," I say.

"Cheeseburger, fries, Coke," says Saul.

"Breakfast Jack, no meat. Cheeseburger, onion rings, root beer, Oreo shake. Extra mayonnaise," I say.

"Hold up. One at a time," she says.

"It's all on the same bill," I say and watch as she licks her lips, her tongue hesitating on the left corner of her mouth.

"Extra mayonnaise on what?" she says.

"On the fuckin' cheeseburger," I say.

"You ain't gotta be talking to me like that," says the woman.

"Okay, check this out." I say. "Cheeseburgers, plural. One with extra mayo. Breakfast Jack, no meat, fries, onion rings, a Coke, a root beer, an Oreo shake, and quit bein' such a motherfucking bitch."

"Oh you ain't seen a bitch yet," she says, her eyes turning to slits. "Y'all come in here all loaded talkin' shit. I ain't gots to take that."

"All loaded?" says Saul.

"I think she just said we was all loaded."

"I think she did."

"I ain't loaded yet. First I'm gonna eat. Then I'm gonna get loaded."

"Yeah," Saul says. "Don't wanna fuck with the high by eating."

"I'm calling the manager," says the woman.

"Now hold up," I say. "You can get all crazy and call the manager. Or you could just serve us our food and we'll be outta here."

"Y'all need to quit talkin' that shit," she says.

I hand her a twenty. "You got the order?"

"Dope fiends comin' up in here talking smack," she mumbles, grabbing the money.

"Is there a problem, Doreen?" asks a pudgy-faced kid in a blue short-sleeved shirt. He's the manager and doesn't have to wear the stupid striped uniform.

"No, sir." Doreen hands me my change and points at a counter with condiments and napkins. "Get your extra mayonnaise over there."

I stare into her eyes as she hands me the bag. "Thanks."

"Woman called us dope fiends," says Saul as he picks up the tray of drinks.

"I know." I grab handfuls of ketchup and mayonnaise packets. "I wonder how she knew?"

"Why you keep lookin' at her like that?"

"Lookin' at her like what?"

"Like you know her."

"I don't know man. She reminds me of someone."

We cross the street and start to walk through the park by the library. In a grassy field behind the baseball diamond a group of kids in uniforms toss a football, getting ready for a game. An old woman sitting on a bench, dressed in a fur coat, drops crusts of bread to the pigeons as a screaming seagull leaps into the air from a light pole and a load of shit lands on the path in front of us as it flies away.

"Ever see people ya know are dead?" I ask Saul.

"Yeah. Every time I look in the mirror."

"No, really, man."

"What? You mean like ghosts?"

"Nah. It's like something someone does, or says, reminds ya of a person you know is dead. But ya can't help but think it's them."

Saul stops walking and stares at me with a worried expression and I realize I'm not explaining myself. The way that woman was licking her lips, how she moved, the way her eyes got small when she talked—it was like someone I used to know. Someone who is dead and gone, but I never saw the body. Only heard about it over the phone. Never seemed real, somebody just saying she was dead and that was it and I'd never see her again.

"That woman behind the counter reminded me of an ex-girlfriend that OD'd."

"And?"

"Just figured it out," I say. "That's why I was staring."

"You're really getting weird, man."

"At least I ain't lookin' in the mirror seeing dead people, motherfucker."

"No," says Saul. "You're just convinced the woman slinging burgers at Jack in the Box is your dead girlfriend reincarnated. Hey, that's normal."

"Forget it, man." I grab the root beer from the tray of drinks Saul is carrying. I lift the lid off the flimsy cup and take a sip. Ice cubes clank against my teeth, the sweet liquid burns my throat. Wiping my mouth with the back of my hand, I return the drink to the tray and heft the bag of food into my arms.

"What the fuck is the deal with them callin' us Hispanics in the newspaper?" says Saul.

"Fuck if I know."

"What? They think nobody in this neighborhood would rob a motherfucker, so they blame it on some Latino from the Mission?"

"Not like you see a lot of yuppies running round pulling stick-ups on Chestnut Street," I say. "Who else they gonna blame?"

"Yeah, but this is our neighborhood. Don't like somebody else getting credit for our shit."

"Hey dude. You're just a predator in the petting zoo."

"What?" says Saul.

"Terrorizing the neighborhood with a brazen string of armed robberies," I say in a deep voice, trying to imitate a local newscaster.

"We'll catch them. It's just a matter of time," says Saul. Then we both laugh.

SOMETHING'S WRONG

SAN FRANCISCO, JANUARY 3, 1997

I take a last drag off the cigarette, and drop it to the sidewalk. I pull the ski mask over my face and walk into the health food store. I approach the checkout counter, slowly slipping the gun from my coat pocket. The salesperson looks up, flinches as I raise the gun to his head.

"Relax," I tell him, and then toss a black gym bag on the counter. "Take all the money, put it in the bag."

The salesperson, a hippie with stringy long hair and beard, stands motionless. Behind him, in the rear of the store, an elderly couple argues about vitamins. To my left, a woman with her back to us opens a refrigerator.

"Hey, don't be stupid. Open the fuckin' cash register and put the money in the bag. Now!"

He pushes a register key and the cash drawer opens. He looks at the money, looks at the gun, and doesn't move. There's the sound of traffic outside, the couple still arguing. The woman closes the refrigerator, a bottle of juice in her hand.

"Hurry up, motherfucker!" I shove his shoulder with the gun.

Hands shaking, he places the money in the open gym bag and steps back. I grab the bag, turn around, and walk out. There's no one on the sidewalk. Cars drive by, but none stop. I slip the mask off, drop it and the gun into the gym bag and begin walking fast. Turning the corner, I pull off my jacket, put it in the bag, and then start running. At the next intersection I slow down and step between two parked cars. I see a cab, hail it, and get in when it pulls over.

"Fillmore and Union," I tell the driver and lean back in the seat. I'm sweating and breathing hard. I want a cigarette. But there's a no smoking sign. A siren screams as a cop car passes going the other direction.

"What time is it?" I ask the driver.

"Three thirty," he answers.

Fuck. I'm late for my therapy appointment.

I never liked to say that Jenny and I were homeless. We'd been evicted from our apartment. I had no job. Jenny had no job. We lived in the camper shell on the back of my pickup truck. Technically, in my mind, the camper was our home. So we weren't homeless. We just didn't have an address.

During the day, while the rest of the world worked, we'd middleman drug deals on 16th Street for a piece of dope, or dumpster dive for recyclables we could turn in for cash. White paper, cardboard, and aluminum brought the most money. Waist deep in giant stinky trash bins behind downtown office buildings, we'd scrape coffee grounds off used Xerox paper and push aside Styrofoam containers looking for aluminum cans. A whole day avoiding rats while separating the good stuff from garbage could net us up to fifty bucks at the recycling yard. Occasionally we'd have to shoplift or steal something that we could trade to the dealers, but that was always our last resort.

At night, after scoring enough dope to keep us well and still have a wake-up shot in the morning, we'd park the truck in an alley along the old China Basin wharf area, stuff all our clothes and assorted weird shit in the truck's cab, and climb in the back and lay down on a futon mattress. It was an airless, claustrophobic space lit by candles and filled with cigarette smoke.

When we had food we'd eat, leaving crumbs in the bed. Occasionally we'd fuck, Jenny's cold feet like small blocks of ice pressed against the backs of my thighs. But most times we'd just lie there, nodding until the candles burned out.

The area on the waterfront where we parked was crawling with wandering crackheads and speed freaks out for a midnight stroll looking for anything to steal. Strange, forgotten street people hovered in doorways so covered in dirt they looked like shadows. When we had to go outside, we went together—and we went as fast as possible.

"There's someone watching me pee," Jenny said.

"Who? That guy over there? He watched me too. It's freezing ,Jenny, come on!"

"I can't piss when someone's watching."

"I'm goin' inside, baby."

"Don't leave me here!" she squealed.

It was as if we were taking a little break from life or on holiday. Sort of like camping. If your idea of the great outdoors includes broken-glass-strewn alleyways filled with stripped cars, used condoms, and hypodermic needles.

Yet there were nights when the locals did more than just watch us. I had to smack a guy in the head with a baseball bat as he tried to break into our camper. And once some lunatics whacked out on meth and living in a car next to ours accused us of being the police and tried to attack us. And then of course there were nights when we had no dope and shivered together, waiting for sunrise so we could begin the day dope sick and looking for some way to score.

I tried to keep my family and friends from knowing we were homeless, but when nobody could reach us because the phone was disconnected, or the mail got returned, everyone knew. I never wanted to admit to myself we were homeless. In my mind we weren't as bad off as we were. We certainly weren't pushing shopping carts like all the crazies we encountered in the streets at night. Yet if we hadn't had the truck we sure as hell would have been.

Those legions of dejected, grime-covered people lying in piss-soaked alleys should have scared me. They were my future. I was fast becoming one of them. How long would it take before I stopped caring about what I looked like? How long before I became just another shadow in the night standing in a doorway, watching the world slip away?

No one in my family could possibly understand. None of them were homeless drug addicts. They were doing well, had homes, were raising families and starting careers. I was envious of how they were living, but I couldn't figure out how the hell they were doing it. They seemed happy and fulfilled. All I had was a sense of futility as everything around me deteriorated. It never occurred to me that they had worked hard to get where they were. I felt as if I was cursed and the world was against me, and Jenny was the only one that understood.

Yet instead of asking for help to try and get ourselves together and off the streets, we continued to live in the back of the truck like it was the normal thing to do. Nodding out night after night, the days blending into weeks, the weeks into months. Time had become meaningless. Something only measured by the amount of drugs we had—the junkie's answer to making everything okay.

Then this garden apartment opened up in my mother's neighborhood. And because I'd been lying to my mother, telling her how good I'd been doing staying off heroin, she offered to help us, pay the first month's rent. And even though it was a little too close in proximity to my family for a couple of dope fiends like us, we accepted. Taking a shit in dark alleys while strangers watched had gotten old.

I never actually met the landlord. Instead, I did an interview over the phone at my sister's house while she was away at work. Some old-sounding guy asked me what I did for a living, what my annual income was, and did I own any pets. I told him I worked construction, made thirty grand a year and had no animals to speak of.

"You sound like a nice young man," he said. "Are you married?"

"My girlfriend and I are engaged," I lied. Across the room Jenny had the end of a belt in her mouth, the other end wrapped tightly around her arm. A perplexed expression appeared on her face as she tried to find a vein with the rig clutched in her hand.

"That's good, that's real good. Sounds like you're making a future for yourself. The apartment is yours if you want it. The other tenants are good people. I'm sure you'll get along. The woman on the second floor is holding a key for you. Just send me a rent check every month."

We took the camper shell off my truck, put it in the backyard, pulled the futon out, tossed it on the bedroom floor, and moved all my stuff from storage. Filling the rooms with boxes of books we'd never read, old clothes, a television, and a kitchen table without any chairs. That first night in our new apartment, lying in bed surrounded by boxes, life was good.

Eight months later the boxes were still there. Some unpacked, most untouched, gathering dust. The futon was surrounded by mounds of dirty clothes, empty bottles, fast-food wrappers, the acidic stench from an overflowing ashtray that lay on the floor in the middle of the bedroom permeated everything. A TV set, constantly on, sat by the door on milk crates. The sink in the kitchen overflowed with dirty dishes. Food-stained paper grocery bags crammed full of garbage piled against the refrigerator. A haze of cigarette smoke hung by the ceiling and four stolen car tires stacked in the living room waited to be sold.

When my mother stopped by and saw how we were living she asked whether I was back on heroin. I assured her that I wasn't. "I'm just having a hard time finding work, I'm a little depressed, and don't feel like cleaning," was what I told her.

"Honey, I'm worried about you," she said.

"Mom, don't worry. I'm fine," I told her. "Can I borrow thirty dollars, use your car this afternoon?"

"There's a woman I know, a therapist. Said she'd see you about your depression. If you want I'll pay for it."

"Sure, mom. I'll see her. Can I get that thirty?"

"You seem to care what your family thinks of you," the therapist says.

Sitting in her office with the black gym bag at my feet, I feel kind of weird. Really, all I want to do is call the dope man, score, and go home. Yet I'm surprised by what the therapist just said. Strangely enough, I do care what they think of me. My lifestyle and actions might make it appear that I don't. But I do.

"Last week you said you've never been fully honest with your mother about your past drug use. How did she find out you were using?"

"That's a long story."

She leans back in her chair and crosses her legs. She's wearing another pantsuit today, this one beige. "We've got time."

I try to remember exactly when my mother first discovered I was a junkie. I've been using for sixteen years, and there's a million possible incidences to consider. Except, of course, yeah, I'd almost forgotten.

Alicia, my soon-to-be ex-girlfriend, was despondent, it being the anniversary of her mother killing herself by jumping in front of a subway train. But I just couldn't relate. All I wanted was more drugs, and I had no time to deal with her grief. We began to argue. She was crying, drinking, and taking pills. And, as usual, talking about killing herself. I ignored her, making phone calls to see if I could middleman us some dope. She started screaming about how nobody cared. Then she fell down, spilling a bottle of purple pills. I tried to take them away. She punched me, knocked over a bookcase. Threw a chair. I told her to go fuck herself, grabbed my coat, and stormed out of the apartment.

After I left she shot more heroin, finished the bottle of whiskey, and swallowed over fifty Xanax. When she realized she was going to fall asleep and never wake up, she changed her mind about dying, called my mother, and asked for a ride to the hospital. Of course my mother went and picked her up, and on the short ride to the emergency room, Alicia, passing in and out of consciousness, managed to tell her we were junkies and had been for years.

The doctors pumped Alicia's stomach and filled her full of charcoal to absorb the rest of the toxic chemicals in her body. Because the drugs were self-administered, they kept her for observation, a legal seventy-two-hour hold on all suicide attempts.

When I returned to our apartment I found my mother sitting at our kitchen table.

"Alicia's told me everything."

"What do ya mean, Mom?"

"Said you guys have been doing heroin. For Christ's sake, Patrick, heroin?"

"I don't know what she told you, Mom. But if ya haven't noticed she's a little out of her mind right now."

"I don't think she's making this up."

"So you believe her instead of me. That's great, Mom. Ya don't even believe your own son."

"I just know what I've seen, and you two haven't been doing so well."

"Things have been kinda hard lately. I'm outta work. I'm depressed, and yeah, I use heroin once in a while. Like, recreationally, ya know? But I ain't no junkie. Alicia has the problem, Mom. Not me."

My mother knew I was lying. Yet she wasn't ready, or able, to admit I was using drugs, especially not heroin. It might have been different if it was cocaine. She wouldn't have been happy about me using coke, but coke doesn't have the negative connotations heroin has. Instead, it was easier for her to blame Alicia, as if Alicia was the one that had led me astray.

Except Alicia wanted to stop using, I didn't.

The hospital released Alicia and there was a lot of confusion. I was caught in the middle, trying to appease everyone. Alicia wanted to quit using and be with me, but only if we stayed off heroin. My mother wanted me to stay off of heroin and stay away from Alicia, and everyone else that I hung out with. And the rest of my family wished I'd get my shit together. As a temporary solution

Alicia went into rehab, and I, with the help of my mother, left San Francisco to live with my older sister in New York City in the hopes that I'd somehow clean up.

I remember Alicia hanging out the window of the rehab yelling that she loved me, saying goodbye and crying. At the time I didn't think anything would ever change, that we'd always be together. Her voice echoes and then fades as I look up and see shadows in the sunlight moving across the ceiling and the therapist is talking, but I'm not listening. Leaning back against the couch I smell the faint odor of perfume left from another client and rub my damp hands along the legs of my pants.

The therapist's office is on Union Street, below the fashionable and upscale Pacific Heights neighborhood, wedged in between the designer clothing boutiques, hair salons, trendy restaurants and bars—the exact same neighborhood I've been robbing. She has a nice clientele. Criminal dope fiends are not her usual patients. The people I meet coming and going from her waiting room are depressed housewives, stressed-out businessmen, and high school kids whose rich parents don't know what to do with them.

The therapist seems okay, mildly liberal, like someone my mother would know. At our first session I sprawled on the couch in her office and told her I'd been depressed for years. She asked about my living situation and my past drug use. My mother had obviously briefed her. I told her the same crap I told everyone—I was clean and had been for some time but was struggling. I agreed to see her on a weekly basis, more to appease my family than anything else.

Now every Thursday afternoon I walk up to Union Street for my appointment. If I'm feeling well I steal a newspaper from one of the kiosks and read the front page before tossing it out. Chain-smoking the entire way, I walk past the shop windows, making mental notes for the future.

Although some days I walk with my head down, so high I can barely make it there. Others, dope sick, I wait for the session to be over so I can go cop. At least once a month I blow it off—I'm too high to remember what day it is, or I'm across town scoring from the dope man.

I don't know what I'm doing at these therapy sessions. I really need to talk to someone. Yet I never talk about the things I need to talk about. I never mention using drugs, or the robberies I'm committing, or my relationship with Jenny, or my mother. I never admit my fears of getting busted. How guilty and crazy I am from having to lie, cheat, and steal from everyone in my life, and the confusion of trying to keep all the lies straight. There's so much I could, and should, talk about, but I don't.

"Are you sleeping at night?" the therapist asks.

"Yeah, why?"

"You're always tired. Just wondered if you were sleeping."

"I sleep," I tell her. "What do you want? I'm depressed."

"What do you mean when you say you're depressed?"

"In the morning, when I wake up, I lay in bed, keeping my eyes closed. I'd rather just sleep all day. There's nothing I want to do. Nothing excites me. I hate everyone. I'd rather be alone. Don't even wanna have sex."

What I failed to mention was that was how I felt before I had my morning shot of dope. I never felt depressed when I was high. It was always afterward, coming down, or when I was sick from withdrawal. Then, my only concern was getting more.

"How would you feel about taking medication?"

"You mean antidepressants?" I respond like it really matters what the medication is. Of course I would take meds. I'm a drug addict. The idea of taking pills to cure my ills appeals to me on so many different levels. "If you think it would help."

"I'll start you on a low dose, then gradually increase it. Remember. You have to give the drugs a chance. They take thirty days to really start working."

Thirty days? What kind of crap is this? The drugs I do work immediately. This antidepressant medication sounds like a bit of a scam. Besides, the prescriptions are ridiculously expensive, and it bothers me that my mother's paying for it. Not that I'm against her buying me drugs, but I'm worried she won't be as generous with other money when I need dope.

The therapist looks up from writing and I notice she's got that concerned expression on her face again.

"Whenever we talk of your parents, you change the subject. You seem to be avoiding something."

"Avoiding something?" I say, somewhat sarcastically.

"We've never discussed your childhood, growing up, or your relationship with your parents when you were younger."

I try not to think about the past. All I can, and want, to focus on is the next shot of dope and where it's coming from. The fear of withdrawal, who I'm going to rob next, and how I'm going to make it through another six hours until I need to shoot more dope is about as complicated as my thoughts ever get.

"There's not much to tell. We moved all the time. One place after another. Different countries, different cities. A lot of places I didn't fit in. My father's a professor of linguistics. I used to joke with my sister that if it was freezing cold and in the middle of an ocean and the local dialect had no known origin, then we lived there. Iceland; the Faroe Islands; Durham, North Carolina; Eugene, Oregon—every couple of years we'd move. I was continually the new kid on the playground. I talked different, I looked different, I felt different."

I rub my temples and close my eyes. I'm with my sister on the outskirts of Torshavn, the town where we lived on the Faroe Islands. As we walk along a dirt path that leads through a sheep meadow to the sea, two older boys appear ahead of us, and when they draw near they stop and say something in Faroese. We look at them and shrug our shoulders, miming with our hands that we don't speak the language. One of the boys becomes visibly agitated and tries speaking in Danish, his face twisted in anger. Again we shrug and I turn away, intent on continuing along the path. Roughly he grabs my shoulder and shakes me. I look up at his face. I don't know what he wants but I can see that he is furious and I'm scared. My sister pulls me free from his grasp and we walk away. A minute later I turn around to look and they're still back there standing and I worry about running into them on our return.

"Are you in contact with your father?" the therapist interrupts.

"We talk every once in a while on the phone. See him when he comes to visit." A murky memory of when I last saw my father creeps into my thoughts. I was so strung out I couldn't sit through dinner at my sister's house. Halfway through I had to leave, go home and shoot more dope. Seems there was something wrong with my legs, because I remember walking with a cane, yet, like the dinner, I can't remember much about it. I hadn't seen my father in a year, but it didn't matter. All I wanted was more drugs. Any sense of family, or caring, was lost. Now, forced to remember, I feel a sense of remorse.

"You look sad. Does thinking of your father make you sad?"

"Nah, I just…I don't know."

"You mentioned a sister. Do you have other siblings?"

"Two sisters. One older, one younger. I'm in the middle."

"Are you in contact with either of them?"

I haven't seen my sister in New York in many years, or if I have I can't remember. My younger sister I see off and on. A couple of times Jenny and I have stayed at her apartment. She and her husband have let us sleep on their hide-a-bed, eat their food, take showers, and watch their TV all night while they sleep.

My head begins to hurt. My mouth is dry and I can taste that metallic taste in the back of my throat, a symptom of early withdrawal. Licking my lips I think of the robbery I just committed. The long-haired salesperson's face flashes across my mind. With the toe of my boot I push the gym bag on the floor by my feet.

"How's your relationship with your mother?"

This is such a loaded question. I don't want to touch it. I'm not really sure how my mother knows this woman. Are they friends, or is she a friend of one of my mother's friends? Does she tell my mother what we talk about? Is it ethical for my therapist to know my mother?

"I get along with my mother," I say. "Although at times I find her to be, ah, intrusive. Like she wants to live my life for me."

"What was she like when you were younger?"

"My mom was a mom. She did all the things moms are supposed to do. She cooked. She cleaned. She read us *The Hobbit* as a bedtime story when we lived on an island in the North Sea. I don't know what you want me to tell you."

"Was she intrusive then?"

"Nah, everything changed when I was twelve. One day my dad was gone. Maybe there was more to it than that. No. Sorry, of course there was more to it than that. But I was a kid. I didn't see it coming."

"How did everything change?"

"My mom took it hard. She checked out, tried to commit suicide a couple of times. Slit her wrists, overdosed on pills. I found her both times—foaming at the mouth, in a pool of blood."

"How did that make you feel?"

"I don't know. I was confused. Mom's in the hospital. No one's telling me anything. Like it was some big secret. I felt lost. I felt like some unwanted fat kid. Hell, my dad left, and my mom obviously didn't want to be there. What was I supposed to feel?"

I suddenly feel angry, and at the same time I feel stupid for being sad. My face feels flush, like I should be crying. But no tears are coming. I want to feel sorry for myself, and feel guilty for being upset at my mother and father. I'm sweaty and cold at the same time and there's a lump in my throat. But it's because I'm jonesing for dope, not because I'm close to tears. I haven't shot up in over five hours.

"I used to have a picture of them," I say, my voice deep, my cadence slow. "Taken right before they separated. My dad's hair is long. He's got a scraggly beard. Seems I remember him in army fatigues, but I think I'm just making that up. And my mom, she's dressed like Jackie O. Looked like Mary Tyler Moore standing next to Che Guevara. I don't know why they ever got together in the first place."

The therapist reaches behind her, produces a box of tissues and tries to hand them to me. I look at her like she's insane. Instead she places them on the floor between us and asks if I was overweight as a child.

"I was what they called husky. At least that's what they called it in boys' clothing. I wasn't good at sports. I hated group activities that were supposed to be fun. I had an undiagnosed learning disability, so I thought I was stupid and couldn't do good in school. My parents left me. Nobody loved me. Hell, I was a mess. Some reason I thought it was all because I was fat. Like being fat made me unlovable and stupid."

I found solace in food. I'd sit and watch TV, shoving candy bars, ice cream, and Fritos in my mouth until I felt sick. Whenever I had to go to the store to do the family grocery shopping, I'd buy a couple of extra things for myself and stash them. *Mmmmm, Del Monte Cling Peaches in Heavy Syrup.* Then I started feeling guilty about eating. I'd throw up and eat more. I didn't even know there was a name for what I was doing. It just sort of came naturally to me. When I started caring about what I looked like to girls it became worse and I tried to starve myself, only to break down and begin the cycle of eating and puking again. I was well on my way to full-blown anorexia when I discovered drugs. Shooting heroin, I could eat anything and be as thin as I wanted.

"I always feel fat," I whisper.

I pass the strange white-noise machine by the door as I leave the office. On my first session I asked her about it. She said it was to maintain a sense of privacy; the hiss and static supposedly made listening to our conversations impossible for someone lurking in the hallway.

The afternoon light has turned golden and even though it's winter, the weather's warm and the sidewalk in front of the therapist's building is full of people.

I heft the gym bag under my arm, move through the crowd. Across the street a taxi slows and pulls to the curb. In front of me, to my right, two men sit on the hood of an unmarked police car. As I near one of them stands and walks directly in my path. A gold shield hangs from a chain around his neck. At his hip, visible for a second when his coat moves, is a holstered 9mm.

"How you doing, my friend?" he asks.

I look at his badge. I look at his face. "Doin' okay," I answer.

The other policeman moves off the car and stands behind me. He's larger than the other cop. His stomach hangs over his belt, straining his T-shirt. "Mind if we ask you a few questions?"

"About what?"

"Like what are you doing here? Where are you going? That sort of thing." The first cop puts his hand on my elbow and firmly steers me toward their car.

"I-I just left my therapist," I stammer. The muscles in my stomach tighten. I shift the gym bag so the majority of it is hidden under my arm.

"Where's your therapist's office?" the second cop asks.

I gesture with my thumb. "Over there."

"What's the address?"

At some point I'd known the address. But now I can't remember. "It's that pink building at the end of the block."

"You don't know your therapist's address?" the first cop says.

"I just go there. I don't need to know the fuckin' address."

"So, you're in the neighborhood to see your therapist?"

"Actually, I live right down the street." I nod in the general direction of my apartment and then wonder if I should have volunteered that information.

"You got some identification that corroborates that?"

I hand over my driver's license. Everyone is staring at us. The second cop reaches into the car's open window and grabs the radio mic. Holding my license in front of his face, he begins reciting my information.

"There's been a lot of problems in the neighborhood." The first cop absentmindedly scratches his crotch. "Been a lot of armed robberies. As a matter of fact, one just happened about ten blocks from here. How long was your appointment with your shrink?"

"Therapist," I correct him. Though I'm not sure why I bother. Maybe I don't want him thinking me insane. Therapists are for dealing with life's problems. Psychiatrists are for crazy people. *Really, Officer, I'm just working on a couple of minor quality-of-life issues.*

"An hour," I say. "I was just leaving when you stopped me. Can I go now?"

"And before that, you were?"

"The gym," I say, slipping the bag from under my arm and pointing at it.

The cop looks at me, unable to immediately respond to a hundred-and-twenty-pound, skinny-as-a-rail, pasty-faced, bags-under-his-eyes junkie who just said he works out at a gym.

"You working on building muscle mass, or just staying fit?" he finally says with a smirk.

"No warrants," the second cop says. The both of them look at each other, and then at me. Shrugging his shoulders, the second cop hands me my license.

"Be seeing you around, O'Neil," the first cop says. "We just got assigned the robbery detail to this precinct. Good luck with all that weightlifting."

WAKE UP

A thundering sound like a subway train screeching to a halt rushes past me and all I can do is lie on the floor with my eyes wide open, wondering what the hell is going on and why these people in uniforms are looking down at me. A plastic mask covers my nose and mouth, and I try to pull it off. A paramedic kneeling next to my shoulder puts her hand out, preventing me from doing so. She wags a finger back and forth and says something, but it's garbled. A walkie-talkie screeches behind me, the distorted dispatcher's voice drowning out whatever the paramedic is trying to tell me. I close my eyes. My head throbs and my body is tense, and I finally understand what's going on.

The paramedic presses her fingers into my wrist. "How ya doing?"

"Don't know," I tell her. Over her shoulder, Jenny talks hurriedly to a man in uniform writing on a clipboard. Her hands flail as she gestures toward me.

All I want to do is go back to sleep. Somewhere comfortable and warm.

"He didn't fucking OD," Jenny is yelling.

"He sure as hell ain't takin' a nap."

I feel pressure on my shoulder and look back at the paramedic's face.

"You with us?" she says.

I feel a prickly sensation creep up the back of my neck. "I'm not goin' nowhere."

"You almost died," she says. "You were out there."

"No I didn't," I say and run my hand across my chest. It feels like someone has been pounding on my rib cage.

"Yes, you did, my friend. Took three shots of Narcaine before we even got a pulse."

The metallic taste in my mouth says she's telling the truth. I'm jonesing. My skin crawls like I haven't shot any dope in days. But that's what Narcaine does. Reverses the effects of opiates. Pulls junkies out of ODs. I've been through this so many goddamn times. Seems I'll never get it right and just go all the way and end this fucking thing for good.

"Been doing CPR for the last ten minutes. It ain't like you was breathin' on your own." Releasing my wrist she pulls the mask off my face and yells to the man talking to Jenny. "He's all right, he'll live. Let's pack up and take 'em for observation."

"Observation?" I say, knowing full well this is the procedure.

"Gotta come with us to the ER," she says.

"He ain't fuckin' going nowhere," Jenny says.

"I appreciate everything you folks have done and all, and don't get me wrong. I'd go with you if I had a way to get back. But SF General is all the way across town."

"You know the drill," says the man. "If ya don't come with us, we call the cops. You want us to radio it in, have the police come over and make out a report, maybe even arrest you?"

A fireman I hadn't noticed before standing in the doorway of our bedroom asks if I can get up and walk, or do I need a stretcher? I sit up. My entire body feels stiff and unresponsive. Mentally, I'm calculating how long this is going to take. The ride over to the hospital, a one-hour observation, filling out the paperwork, getting released, and then the bus ride back. It's not looking good. With the Narcaine flowing through my blood stream, in less than an hour, I'll be in full withdrawal.

"Can I get a cigarette?" I ask, shifting my eyes at Jenny.

"The man almost dies and the first thing he wants is a cigarette. There just ain't no justice," says the paramedic, shaking her head and packing up her gear.

"There's no smoking in the ambulance."

"We ain't in the ambulance."

"You wanna do this the hard way?" says the man in uniform. "Call the fucking cops. I ain't playing with this motherfucker."

The fireman starts talking into his radio and I tell him to hold on, it's okay. No need to get crazy, man. I just wanted a cigarette. Jenny hands me my leather jacket and starts pulling on her hooded sweatshirt. Then she grabs the cigarettes and a ring of keys. Touching my shoulder she tells me it's all right, we'll do this quick and come right back home.

There's nothing quick about San Francisco General. Once you're in their system it takes forever to get back out. Every intern, orderly, doctor, and nurse at the ER knows I'll just sit there biding my time, waiting for them to cut me loose so I can go shoot more dope, and they'll keep me for as long as possible, locked up in some examination room off the side of the ER. If they really got it bad for me they'll fill out the 5150 forms claiming I'm a suicide attempt and then turn me over to the psych ward for a seventy-two-hour evaluation.

One time back when I was still with Alicia and we were dope sick, drinking booze and taking pills, I slipped on the stairs coming down out of our loft and fell into the window. Almost made it all the way through to fall two stories into the air well but instead got impaled on the shards of glass stuck in the window frame. Cut up and covered in blood, I pulled myself free and then decided to go back to bed and lie down. Next thing I know there's paramedics and cops and they're pulling me out from under the covers, dragging me off to General.

A local anesthetic, some forty-odd stitches, and a couple of hours later a do-gooder intern is asking me what happened, and I'm still so wasted I think he's asking if Alicia had something to do with it and I tell him it was self-inflicted. I don't know why. It just sort of sounded good at the time and god knows I really wasn't lying.

Well, you can probably guess the rest. Right after he hands me a pair of crutches these two really large dudes appear and walk me across the hall to the psych ward. I'm telling any and everyone that will listen, and a few that won't, this is all a big mistake. I really don't belong here. Then this cold-looking bitch in white with short-cropped blond hair tells me to sit down, the doctor will see me when she's ready.

It has to be about six in the morning and there's a couple guys sitting around a lounge area looking at a TV set, but mostly they're staring off into space. In the corner some girl's got her face shoved against the wall and she's yelling about microwaves invading her head, while two older-looking wino dudes are playing checkers and laughing. Then an orderly comes in with a bunch of meals on these insulated trays and the place goes crazy. Everyone is grabbing food and yelling. Feeding time at the loony bin.

An hour later the psychiatrist arrives and looks me over and starts asking questions—but from the expression on her face it's obvious she's pretty much convinced I'm out of my mind. I just want to go home, I tell her. She asks me why, is there something wrong? And I bite and tell her I'm not crazy and I don't belong here. Then she asks who said I was crazy. I said look where I am. And she asks do I know where I am and why I'm here. And that's when I just stop talking, 'cause this is going nowhere and everything I say sounds insane.

Two hours later—in pain, dejected, and thoroughly depressed—I'm standing by a door with no handle and one of those two-inch-wide vertical reinforced glass windows running down the upper half of it, and out in the hall people are walking by. I see Alicia and our friend Don, and I start banging on the door. She turns and sees me and just shoves the breaker bar emergency handle and it opens. She grabs me, and we're running down the hallway into the bright light of day as an alarm sounds behind us.

"Babe, you all right?"

"What?" I look into Jenny's eyes and we're outside by the ambulance. "Fuckin' freezing. Need a cigarette." Behind me are two fire trucks, their lights flashing away in the night, out in front of our apartment building.

"How ya doin', sport?" says a paramedic as he opens the ambulance's back door.

"Been better," I mumble and start to get in. "All right if I catch a quick smoke before we take off?"

"Just hold up on that," says the woman paramedic, walking toward us carrying a large black nylon bag. The firemen behind her turn toward their vehicles, one of them laughs and I'm sure he's laughing at me.

"He coulda smoked one already," Jenny says, an annoyed pout plastered across her face.

The woman paramedic stands in the middle of the street clutching her bag and glares at Jenny. "You know you ain't the one being taken to the hospital. I could not let you come along for the ride. So please shut up."

Nobody says anything and we all stand in the street by the back of the ambulance looking at one another. Jenny looks at me, shrugs, turns to the woman paramedic. "Whatever."

"Haven't we met before?" says the other paramedic, holding the door open and gesturing for us to get inside.

I look at him. He doesn't look familiar. Nothing does. Everything has this fuzzy edge, and all the lights are way too bright.

He points to Jenny. "Didn't you have a problem with some Valiums?"

"Valiums? Like Valiums would be a fuckin' problem."

"Nah, nah, they were pills you thought were Valiums."

Something about this is starting to sound familiar. A long time ago Jenny had taken some little blue pills thinking they were Valiums and then an hour later she started doing all these spastic contortions. Trying to curl her body backward. Her head touching her toes as her back arched like a distempered cat.

"Yeah, they were psych meds, remember?" I turn to the paramedic. "You picked us up and drove us to the hospital and all we needed was some Benadryl to combat the side effects."

The paramedic nods his head. "Those pills do some nasty things."

"Never happened," says Jenny as she steps into the ambulance. "Can we get this over with?"

"That was fuckin' weird," I say.

"Never forget a face or a drug-induced complication," says the paramedic, his hand on my elbow helping me through the door. "Watch your step."

"I hate to cut y'all's beautiful reunion short," the woman paramedic starts, "but we got a long drive to General and a whole lotta other calls to make before the night is over."

"Love you too," I say and lie on the gurney.

As we roll into the hospital parking lot, I sit up to look out the window and see three other ambulances, some cop cars, and a group of people in various uniforms standing around the emergency room's entrance. An orderly and a security guard walk up to the driver's window and ask our paramedic what she's got. When she tells them it's an OD and I'm alive and just here for observation they laugh and tell her she's at the back of the line and it's going to be a few hours. There are gunshot wounds, stabbings, a woman giving birth, and two attempted suicides in front of us.

"You wanna smoke?" she asks as she turns around in her seat rubbing the side of her face with her fingertips. "Go ahead, kill yourself some more. Looks like we got time."

"Cool, thanks," I say and step out the back of the van.

Jenny hands me a cigarette and lighter. "Ain't this a bitch."

"It's like a goddamn dead people's convention, huh?" I say and then give her a light.

Jenny brushes her hair out of the way and I look at her in the glow of the lighter's flame and think how beautiful she is. "That's not funny," she says. Her eyes glistening, she glances away and wipes her face with her hand. "You almost died."

The cigarette tastes incredibly good as I inhale the smoke deep into my lungs. Putting my arm around Jenny, I lean my head down on her shoulder and stroke her hair. "You know nothing's gonna kill me. I've OD'd six, okay, seven times already. If it was gonna happen, it would've happened. I'll live forever, baby."

"You weren't breathing. Your lips were blue."

I tell her it's okay, that I love her and not to worry. Standing together in the shadow of the ambulance, I hold her in my arms and we stay that way for a long time, until a man walks up asking us for a cigarette and I tell him to fuck off.

"What the fuck are we doin'?" I say to Jenny. She just shakes her head and takes another drag. "Let's get out of here."

I grab Jenny's hand and we walk across the parking lot, weaving our way between the ambulances and police cars. With every step the noise lessens, the garish lights grow dimmer, until we walk out the gate and the shadows of the night engulf us.

A few of the neighboring houses have their lights on, but most are dark and silent. There's nobody around. Nothing else here but a closed liquor store, turned-over trashcans, and walls covered in graffiti. I can see traffic passing a block away on Potrero Avenue and we start walking in that direction.

I can hear someone shouting behind us, but I don't turn around. Somewhere in the near vicinity a dog howls. A siren is getting closer. I let go of Jenny's hand, wrap my jacket around me and keep walking.

Something's burning, I can smell it in the air. A fire truck flies through the intersection, its horn blaring and lights flashing. At the corner there's a bus stop with a payphone and as Jenny stands at the curb looking for a bus I call the dope man's pager and hang up.

Just Say No

Rain splatters against the panaderia's window. On the table in front of me there's a cup of cold coffee, pastry crumbs, a crumpled napkin, six empty sugar packs, and a dusting of white sugar granules into which I've scrawled the word FUCK.

The rain comes down so hard I can barely see out the window. At my feet is a gym bag. In my coat pocket, a gun. I'm wearing a pinstriped suit under a black raincoat. My hair is slicked back. Large aviator sunglasses, the lenses light yellow, partially cover my face. I have no money. I'm out of cigarettes. I have no more dope, and Jenny's at home waiting for me.

Last year, when Saul was still around, we'd cased the bank across the street but never robbed it. It's a small branch of a major firm in a shitty neighborhood. There's a counter along the back with three teller windows and a small area by the door with two chairs and a coffee table, and if I remember right, a large fake potted plant by the window. The couple of times I've been inside, the place was near empty and unless some dramatic change has happened I'm hoping it's business as usual and I'm their only customer.

Last night, intent on holding up a local liquor store, I walked outside and stopped, breathed the night air, and knew if I stuck a gun in somebody's face the cops would be there. Standing on the sidewalk I lit a cigarette and played all the possible scenarios in my mind. None came out with me getting away.

Tossing the cigarette into the gutter, I turned around, went back inside. Jenny looked up as I opened the door. When I took off my jacket and sat on the bed, she asked me what was going on. I told her if I robbed somebody tonight I was going to get busted. She looked at me strange. Went back to watching TV. And I just sat there feeling like things were happening I had no control over.

This morning I shot the remainder of the dope, put on a suit, and walked out the door. If this was going to be my last holdup, I sure as hell wasn't going out robbing some liquor store for a couple hundred dollars.

Covering my head with the gym bag, I run across the street and duck into the entrance of a vacated store two doors down from the bank. With the wind still throwing rain at me, I step further into the back of the building's portico. I run fingers through my hair and try to straighten my appearance. Over my shoulder I catch sight of two disheveled men huddled at the entrance with their backs to me. I take off my glasses and squint at them.

"Ya just go inside. Show 'em the note," the taller of the two whispers. "It's easy."

Startled, I turn to see if he's talking to me. Realizing he isn't, I step further back into the shadows.

"They read the note, hand ya the money, and then we're gone," he continues.

"I'm scared, Dan," the shorter of the two whines.

"That's not what ya said last night."

They're both soaking wet, dressed almost identically in dark Levi's and dirty white tennis shoes, and wearing baseball caps backward on their heads. The taller one smokes a cigarette while moving his jaw back and forth. The shorter one, shuffling from one foot to another, bops up and down as if he's running in place.

"I done a mess a shit," he whispers, "but robbing a bank?"

"Ain't nuttin' to it," the one called Dan says.

"How you know? You never done it."

"Feller in county told me how." Dan cupped his hands conspiratorially in front of his mouth. "'Sides, ya use a note, ain't as bad as usin' a gun. Ain't even a felony."

He takes another cigarette and lights it using the end of the one he's been smoking. The sound of rain hitting the pavement echoes in the confined entrance. As the smoke drifts toward me, I feel drawn to it, and step forward.

"Actually," I say, "what you need to worry about is if the person you're robbing feels he's being threatened or that his life is in danger." The two of them turn, startled. The shorter one looks ready to run. "That's an additional charge the DA can consider when prosecuting. But all robberies, whether there's a gun or not, are felonies. Got an extra cigarette?"

"Who the fuck are you?" Dan asks, the shorter one shuffling over until he's behind Dan.

"Just stopped in here to get out of the rain," I answer. "Couldn't help overhearing your conversation. Can I get a smoke, Dan?"

He hands me a cigarette. "You a lawyer?"

The short guys squeals, "You the police?"

Dan shoots him a sideways glance, his eyes narrow slits.

"No, just know a little 'bout robberies," I answer.

A large puddle begins forming on the sidewalk in front of us as water from the gutter overflows the curb. A small wave caused by a passing car crashes at our feet. The wind blows, the rain continues to fall. The three of us stand together in silence. Without a word the two of them take off running in the opposite direction of the bank.

I watch the rain while finishing my cigarette. Savoring the last puff, I drop the smoldering filter to the ground and head to the bank. I push open the door and walk inside, water dripping off me. Save for the lone teller behind the counter, the room is deserted.

"Good afternoon." I point my gun at her. "Don't do anything stupid. Put the money in the bag, and I'll be on my way."

The woman looks at me and chews her gum. From the cash drawer she takes out a small stack of twenties and places them in the gym bag I've spread open on the counter in front of her. Then she pulls out a handful of loose bills and two rolls of quarters and lays them alongside the twenties and stares at me.

"More," I say.

The woman keeps staring. She's looking me in the eyes, which is odd. Most people stare at the gun, or at the floor, but never directly into my eyes. Placing her hands, palms down, on the counter she licks her lips, pauses, and says no.

"No?" I say. "What the fuck you mean no?"

"I'm not giving you any more money," she says.

I don't know how to respond. No one has ever said no. I've had people cry and beg me to go away. I've watched people completely break down and give me every bit of money they could get their hands on. One time there was a teller that freaked out so bad he ducked behind the counter and wouldn't come up—had to reach over into the cash drawer myself. But I've never had anybody just flat out say no.

"Bitch," I mumble, grab the bag, and walk out the door. The rain is coming down in sloshing wet curtains. I'm immediately soaked and there are no cars, no buses, and no taxis. The street is virtually deserted.

I step off the curb and sink past my ankle into a deep puddle. Struggling to cross the street I slip on the wet pavement and almost fall before making it to the other side. As I pass the panaderia I look through the window at the mess I left on the table. Steam forms on the glass, and it looks warm inside. At the corner I turn, walk half a block, duck into an alley, and step into an alcove hidden by a dumpster. I quickly take off my suit. I'm wearing black jeans and a T-shirt underneath, and I toss the wet clothes into the dumpster along with the empty gym bag. Slipping the wet raincoat back on, I put the money in my pocket and stuff the gun in the waist of my pants. I pull a knit cap onto my head, toss the glasses, and leave the alley.

A man eyes me as I make my way toward him. "Spare change?" he says. The shopping cart full of clothes and the bedroll next to him are completely drenched as the rain continues to come down. Ignoring him, I walk across the street.

A cop car speeds toward me with its lights on. It slows as the cops inside look me over, then keep driving. I walk into a store and buy a pack of cigarettes. Coming out I see cops in front of the bank. My hands are trembling and I flag an approaching taxi.

"Where to?" the driver says.

"Haight and Fillmore."

"Something jumpin' off back there," he says and jerks his thumb in the direction of the police cars.

"Yeah, must be," I say.

"I just don't get it," the driver says. "How much could you possibly get pulling a robbery?"

I begin to say something but remain silent instead.

"Is it really worth going to prison?" he continues. "You either gotta be desperate or outta your mind."

The driver is starting to piss me off. I want to tell him he's an ass, pull out the money and wave it in his face. Like that would make any sense. Shoving my hands into my coat pocket I touch the rolls of quarters. The teller's face as she mouths "no" plays over and over in my mind. The anger begins to fade.

"You going to a specific address or will the corner do?" he says.

"Right here's fine," I say and hand him a twenty as he pulls over. "Keep the change," I mumble and get out.

Perchance to Dream...

The dope man won't come to our house. Even the lure of selling a quarter ounce won't get him here. Some nights he's like that. Instead we make plans to meet in the Haight. I tell Jenny I'll be back in a while. I take the .38 from my desk and slip it inside my coat pocket.

The wind from the Bay cuts through me as I wait for the bus. Across the street my neighbor comes home. The automatic door opens and he effortlessly drives his Range Rover into the garage. I can hear a television from one of the apartments in a nearby building. Someone laughs and I curse them under my breath for having a good time. I've only enough money for dope and a bus ride. Every couple of days I have to pull another robbery.

The bus takes forever. My stop comes and I wander to a pay-phone to call the dealer.

Twenty minutes later I'm back at the bus stop. My leather jacket is useless against the cold, the lining is torn, and the zipper's broken. I pull out my cigarettes and realize I'm almost out. I count the change in my pocket. I don't have enough for another pack. I barely have the bus fare. The muscles in my chest tighten. I feel anxious and sweaty. The weight of the gun pulls at my jacket, and I'm conscious of it being there.

When I get on the bus I sit in the back by the window. In front of me are three kids, they look like gangbangers, but it's hard to be sure. One of them pushes the other and he falls across the aisle onto an older woman who's holding a bag of groceries. She screams and the driver stops the bus. "Gonna call the cops if y'all don't stop messin' 'round!"

"Man, fuck you," says one of the kids.

Then he sees me staring. "What-a-ya lookin' at fool?"

The driver turns the steering wheel, the bus shimmies as he weaves through traffic. The kid glares in my direction, then looks away. A few minutes later all three get up and stand by the back door. The woman with the groceries moves away from the center aisle. The driver pulls to the curb and they begin filing out.

"Fuck you, bitch," the kid says as he flips me off.

My anxiety turns to anger. I close my eyes and dream of shooting the kid—his brains splattering across the interior of the bus. I replay the image over and over, nonstop, until it's not the kid anymore, it's me, and a cop smiling as he pulls the trigger, the bullets ripping through my chest. I suck in my breath and open my eyes. I've been having vivid dreams of getting shot. In bed, when I close my eyes, I see cops, their guns pointing at me, the smell of cordite and blood in my nostrils.

A strong gust of wind blows dust in my face as I get off the bus. On the corner is a payphone. I dial the number to my house. After three rings Jenny picks up.

"I'm fuckin' losing it," I tell her.

"What happened?"

"Some punk kid on the bus."

"Is that all? Thought dude didn't show with the dope. Come on, baby. Don't let some kid bother you."

She's right. I know she's right. I lean my head against the side of the booth as I relax my grip on the phone.

"Where are you?" she asks.

"On the corner, almost home."

"We need cigarettes and cat food."

"The cat needs food?"

"Cats eat," says Jenny.

"I ain't got…"

"What?" she says.

I want to tell her I don't have any more money. I want to tell her I'm cold and I just want to come home. I want to tell her I'm tired of pulling robberies. I'm scared shitless. I'm getting anxiety attacks. I'm dreaming of police shooting me.

I hang up the phone.

In the middle of the block there's a small market where I buy cigarettes. I pull out the gun as I walk inside. The woman behind the counter stares and doesn't move. A Chinese language program plays on a small black-and-white television beside her.

"Gimme a carton of Camels, cat food, and all the money," I tell her.

"I know you," she says.

"Camels, money, cat food," I yell, my head feeling like it's going to explode.

"You live neighborhood. You buy from me," she says, holding her hands up in the air. "Why you do this?"

I point the gun at her face and say nothing. She opens the cash register, pulls out money, and grabs a carton of Camel Filters and puts it all in a bag and hands it to me. "Cat food over on shelf."

LOOKING BACK:
ANXIETY'S GREATEST HITS

I'm in a dark, trash-filled alley between tall brick buildings. Two men stand in the shadows. I can't see their faces. I hand one of them money and he gives me the dope. There's a light coming from an open window. There's music and someone crying. I'm happy I'm going to get high. I'm in a room stuck facedown between the bed and the wall. I hear someone coming. I want to yell, but I can't. I'm having trouble breathing. I try to move. Behind me a door creaks open. I can't turn around. I know they're standing there. I scream…

I sit up in bed, gasp for air, and check to see if I still have the drugs in my hand. The lights are off and the TV is on with the sound turned down. Jenny pulls her arm off me, an annoyed look on her face as she rolls over. The cat, curled in a ball, lifts its head and yawns.

I light a cigarette, run my hand across my chin, and lie back against the pillows. I'm covered in sweat. The sheets are wet and my heart pounds inside my chest. The light from the TV bathes the room in a bluish glow. I blow smoke at the shadows that play across the walls. It's 3 AM, and all I want to do is go back to sleep.

I reach over and touch Jenny, the warmth of her body somehow calming. In the metal box by the side of the bed is a small piece of dope we've saved for our morning wake-up shots. I quietly break off half into the spoon.

Jenny lifts her head and opens her eyes. "What's the matter?"

"I can't sleep."

"Ohhhh," she slurs.

Within seconds her breathing slows. I tie off my arm and press the rig into my flesh, waiting for the rush. But nothing comes. The amount of dope is so miniscule I can't feel it.

I walk to the bathroom to take a piss. The medicine cabinet is slightly ajar and I see my reflection in the mirror. I stare at my face, unable to comprehend who I'm looking at. As if it's me looking out from a different face. Yet there's a dullness to the eyes. A dullness I've seen before.

"Can you identify the deceased?" asks the cop. Even in the morgue I can smell his bad breath as he hovers beside me.

"Yeah, that's him," I say, looking at the partially covered body.

"'Him' as in?" asks the other cop, who every time he looks in my direction his expression says he wants to kick the living shit out of me.

"That's Chris." Although, as I look into his dull dead eyes staring up from the gleaming stainless-steel table, it's hard to actually say it is my best friend lying there dead.

I thread my way through the maze of dirty clothes and half-filled boxes that crowd the living room and sit down on a chair. The cat walks out of the bedroom and rubs against my leg. It looks up as I pet its head, then moves off toward the kitchen. I grab my overcoat off the floor and wrap it around me.

Another sleepless night in a cold damp motel room. The electric wall heater, its glowing red heating element visible through the vent, blows damp warm air toward me, but I can't feel it. I hear the rain falling against the window. The room is dark and the curtains are drawn. I'm sitting on a double bed, the polyester comforter a dark blue. There's a gun in my hand. The safety is off. There's a bullet in the chamber. My finger on the trigger, I raise the gun, put the barrel in my mouth. I taste gun oil. I hear the rain. I lower the gun as tears run down my face.

The wind blows through the trees in the backyard. There's the sound of footsteps above me, someone walking in one of the apartments upstairs.

"You okay?" Jenny is standing next to me wearing a large T-shirt. She leans her skinny body against me, puts her hand on my shoulder. "What are you doing out here?"

"Can't sleep."

"Come to bed," she says, walking toward the bedroom.

"In a minute."

The cat runs out of the kitchen licking its lips, pauses, then runs after Jenny. The sound of the TV drowns out the wind. I hear the strike of a lighter.

What the fuck am I going to do? Can't keep doing these robberies. Can't keep shooting dope. Goddamn methadone clinic wants as much money as it takes for us to get well. What's the difference? One drug for another, and I still have to come up with cash in the end.

I think about the dope I just did and want more. But this time I want to feel it. I want to feel it like I haven't felt it in a very long time.

"What time is it?"

"Four o'clock, babe. Come to bed."

"Need a smoke Jenny."

"Well fuckin' come get one. Ain't your servant."

"Think I'm losing my mind."

"Babe. Shut the fuck up and come to bed."

"Hey O.G., got any pills?"

"Got some Dolaphine."

"What you want for 'em?"

"Two each."

"Give me ten," I say and hand him a twenty. He's trying to beat me, but I put my hand out anyway. Nine fat, aspirin-looking pills fall into my hand and I stand there holding them with my palm out. "Hey, old man. I don't know what this is, but they sure as hell ain't no Dolaphine."

"Tha's Dolaphine."

"Man, this ain't even Codeine. Give me my motherfuckin' money back."

The old man moves, I feel something pull at my jacket and step back, spilling the pills onto the sidewalk. There's a slice across the front of my leather jacket, the torn lining sticking out through the hole. The old man stands a few feet away, a small knife in his left hand.

"You gonna stab me over twenty dollars?"

"I'll stab you over five." He's twitching and looking crazy, like he really might be insane.

"Old man, you outta your fuckin' mind," I say and step toward him. A girl with a baby standing in a doorway yells there's gonna be a fight. Two youngsters come running and ask the old man if he's okay. More people start coming.

I turn and walk away.

"Yeah, motherfucker," says the old man.

The cat jumps into my lap and startles me. "Remember that old man tried to stab me?"

"That old man in the Tenderloin?"

"Yeah, just thought about him."

"Why you think 'bout that?"

I get up and go into the bedroom. Jenny's in front of the TV, she looks like a corpse in its muted glow. I ask for the cigarettes, but she doesn't move.

"I gotta go," says Saul.

"Go where, man?"

"Back to Iowa, I guess."

"Iowa?"

"Yeah, fuckin' Iowa."

"What the fuck's in Iowa, Saul?"

"Hopefully not heroin."

I look down at the bed and see the impression my body has crushed into the futon. Two years of lying there nodding away. Cigarette burns dot the blankets. A used rig lies discarded on the floor.

I'm going to die in this fucking bed.

Sitting in a bar on the Lower East Side, drinking a Dewar's on the rocks, and reading the *New York Times*.

December 24th. Merry fucking Christmas.

Critic's Notebook; Reflections on a Punk-Rocker's Death

By Robert Palmer

The news came in a plain white envelope marked "personal and confidential." "Will Shatter died last Wednesday," it said. "He married in November and his wife is expecting their child. Flipper always appreciated your reviews; thought you would want to know."

Flipper, the San Francisco rock band Will Shatter sang, played bass, and wrote songs for, had a special relationship with its audience. Some listeners felt that Flipper was the heart and soul of American punk rock, and that Mr. Shatter was the heart and soul of Flipper. During the band's early days, the West Coast punk scene was steeped in a raging nihilism that all too often turned in upon itself...

"Man, we've seen this movie already."

"Nothin' else on," says Jenny.

The bed is still damp, the scent of my sweat everywhere. I take a drag off the cigarette, the smoke tasteless as it fills my lungs.

Wish this fucking night would end.

I watch Jenny as she smokes. It's as if she's wasting away, getting older before my eyes. Yesterday, when she kissed me and then tried to climb on top, I told her to get off. I just don't want anyone touching me. The feel of her skinny body reminded me of how hard-looking she's becoming. I can't help but feel some distorted fucked-up sense of responsibility. All of this is my doing. I'm the older one. I should know better. Where's she going to go if I'm not around? What's she going to do? How am I supposed to be taking care of her when I can't even take care of myself?

I feel like I should be crying but no tears are coming. I lean forward and start rocking back and forth.

"Babe, you all right?"

"I'm sorry," I say.

"Sorry? Sorry for what?"

"Sorry everything's so fucked up."

"Aw, babe, it's gonna be okay."

"You know I care about you, right?"

"I know you do."

"Maybe we should get on Methadone?"

"You wanna?" says Jenny, a strange worried look on her face.

"Not really. But what else we gonna do?"

"It'll work out. It always does."

"I'm just tired, Jenny. Sorry."

"Get some sleep."

"Dolan's coming in the morning."

"Okay, babe."

LAST DAY – REVISITED

SAN FRANCISCO, JUNE 25, 1997, 2:30 PM

In the car coming back from the robbery I tell Dolan I've got a feeling my time is up. Either I'm going to get busted, or the cops are going to shoot me. Between drags on my cigarette I tell him I haven't been sleeping at night. And every time I nod out on dope I come to with a jolt freaking out, short of breath. He looks at me as if I'm damaged. I don't know if he believes me. But it really doesn't fucking matter. I'm so tired from not sleeping. My words are halted, my thoughts jumbled and confused. Instead of taking the usual precautionary measures of ditching the car outside my neighborhood to throw the cops off, we park two blocks away, because both of us are lazy and don't want to walk any farther than that.

When we get home Jenny's in the bedroom. I grab the telephone and punch in the dope man's number, my whole body stiff with anxiety. "How'd it go?" she asks, like we just came home from a hard day's work or something. I ignore her. I know we fucked up. I really don't want to tell her how we got boxed into a parking place by a bus. Or that the woman who worked the ticket booth of the theater we'd robbed had followed me into the street screaming and pointing as her neighbors hurried outside to see what all the commotion was about. At least three or four of them had gotten a really good look at my face before Dolan was able to get us out of there, maneuvering the car through the afternoon traffic, running the red light.

The dope man's paging service answers. I leave my number and hang up, muttering about always having to wait for drugs. I take off my jacket and shirt and pull off my shoes and socks. The only piece of clothing I have left on is my pants, so loose they barely stay up on my waist.

Dolan sits down, lights a cigarette, stares at the floor.

Jenny, noticing that we aren't exactly celebrating, asks what's wrong and I mumble that it didn't go so well. The phone rings. It's the dope man, says he'll be here in ten minutes, asks how much dope we want, then hangs up with a grunt.

"How long he say it'd take?" Jenny asks, referring to the dealer, and then as an afterthought, before I can answer, she says, "What do you mean it didn't go so well?"

"I blew it, babe." I pull the pile of loose bills out of the bag I'm carrying them in. A quick count tells me I only snagged four hundred dollars, a hundred and fifty of which I hand Dolan. Between drags on his cigarette he recounts the money, then folds it into a wad and stuffs it into his pocket.

I take the gun out of my jacket on the floor, walk over to the closet, and stick it in the hole in the wall behind the shelves. I turn around just as the doorbell rings. All three of us look up in unison. Jenny opens the door, then goes out to let the dope man in through the locked door in the alleyway.

Within minutes the transaction is done. We're back in the bedroom before he's even closed the door behind him. And then it's open the bags, cook the dope, put a needle in my arm. It takes all of two minutes. Bought ten Klonopins as well as the four grams of heroin. I pop three of those and walk into the living room looking for a cigarette. Dolan isn't there and I say something to Jenny. Ask if she knows where he went. I'm half naked, nodding out, and there's a trail of blood running down my arm from where I just shot up. Looking around for something to wipe it off with, I hear a knock at the door. Thinking it's Dolan, I reach for the doorknob.

INTERLUDE

"Only those who can leave behind everything they have ever believed in can hope to escape."

— *William S. Burroughs*

ALMOST HOME

Up on Sixteenth Street, above Market, there's a large, three-story Victorian, a highly coveted piece of San Francisco real estate. My friend Will Shatter OD'd there over twenty years ago. I usually drive by the place on my way across town. It's getting so I don't even think about it anymore. There was a time I didn't know how I felt about Will dying, the way his wife found him crumpled up against the stove in the kitchen. About how he fell down after he did his last shot. Lights out.

I'd been out of town when it happened. Before I left we'd made some sort of vague promise that we'd both quit shooting dope. Then I moved to New York City and the next thing I'm getting a phone call saying Will's dead, then reading his obituary in the *Times*.

A few days ago I thought I saw Will walking across Market Street. He had a certain gait, skinny legs, always looked cool. He even got away with having a receding hairline. There was something intriguing, almost enticing, about Will. Something more than the fact that he sang and played bass in a band. Women were attracted to him. I hated to hang out with him at the clubs, because when I did, they never paid any attention to me.

Sitting in my car at a stoplight, I watched the person I thought was Will walk into a bar, a bar I'd been to before—back when I knew Will, back when I was using, back before he killed himself.

The phantoms and apparitions are everywhere. Sometimes—depending on my frame of mind, how well I've been taking care of myself, whether I'm overworked, lack of sleep, bad diet, tired—that's when I see them the most. Out of the corner of my eye, hanging out in doorways, are faded visions that when I stop and stare aren't there at all.

Most of the people I considered my friends and used drugs with are dead and gone. Yet I remember each and every one as if I'd just laid eyes on them. Even though I know they've passed away, I keep thinking I'll see some of my old friends again and inadvertently catch a glimpse of something familiar in someone else. The way people walk and talk and carry themselves, the expressions on their faces remind me of the dead.

There've been times I'd have to tell myself they're not here anymore. Unless I've actually found someone dead, with a needle still sticking out of his arm, or identified the body at the morgue, or gone to an open-casket funeral, it's like the death isn't real. Unless I've touched their arteries and found no pulse, checked airways to be sure they're not breathing, or seen the fatal wound first hand, it's like they're just not around right now, but someday they might be. I might see them at the flea market, buying cheap pairs of socks, looking like they just got out of bed. Or maybe I'll run into them some night down at a Chinese restaurant digging into a bowl of fried rice.

The city itself haunts me. Whether I'm looking up from reading the newspaper while riding the bus or driving home from work, spectral landmarks leap out at me: a passing street corner; an apartment building where someone I've known has died. General

Hospital, the Hall of Justice, County Jail, the Pontiac Hotel, that subsidized housing project off of 3rd Street that I used to live in, all of them are vertical graveyards. Rooms, apartments, and jail cells, nothing but stacked gravesites, their blank windows aligned and symmetrical like tombstones.

People ask me how I can live in a city where so many of my friends have died, where I got high for twenty years. And all I can tell them is that I've shot dope in every major city in America and Europe. What's the difference? Time diffuses the past and mutes memories. Friends fade from my thoughts and I keep on living.

These days I can be at an intersection where I used to meet my dealer and don't even think of the hours I spent waiting there for drugs to be delivered. I don't think of the endless afternoons of dope-sick withdrawals, nursing a drink in a bar or staring at a cold cup of coffee in some rundown café. It was a long time ago. I shot dope, sold drugs, did crimes, went to jail. It doesn't mean I have to continue living like that.

Three months ago, at the café down the hill from my house, I ordered my usual latté, and looked out the front window onto Grant Street. I thought I saw Sweet walking in front of the saloon across the street. There he was, strolling by and getting into a white van. Just like the white van of his I sold for his sister after he died.

His was one of those deaths where I saw the body. My flatmate Mia and I had been out all night driving around the city when we realized we hadn't seen him in days. Something clicked. At a badly lit intersection by the railroad tracks, I turned the car around and drove home. We found him in his loft, in bed, under the electric blanket. He'd been dead for two days. His room smelled putrid, his body bloated and stiff.

I woke up our other roommates and somebody called an ambulance. We huddled together in the kitchen, not looking at one
another. Mia was crying. But I couldn't feel anything—too much
dope in my veins. When the operator found out the person in question was dead, she told us to wait for the coroner and then hung up.
I got angry that none of my other roommates had done anything,
noticed the smell, checked to see if Sweet was all right. I'd been
downstairs in my room for the last couple of days, high and out of it.
I hadn't thought to check in on him either. He had come downstairs
and told me he wasn't feeling well, borrowed a couple bags of tea and
some honey, said goodnight, and went to bed.

When the coroner showed up, before he even saw the body, he
looked at us and asked if it was a drug overdose. Shrugging my
shoulders, I said I didn't know. Everyone else looked at me like I
should.

"I wasn't living his life," I said, then turned around and walked
downstairs to my room. Lost in "what ifs," I sat in the dark for at
least an hour. If I had just gone upstairs to check in on him I might
have saved him, found him before he died. I'd been in my room,
directly below his, while he passed away. I'd been too high to care,
too preoccupied even to walk up a flight of stairs. Too wasted,
wound up, and unwilling.

So I shot some more dope.

Hours later, the doorbell rang. The medical examiners, paramedics, and police had arrived. They marched up the stairs.
The sound of their voices, the thud of their boots, the collective
squawking of their radios jolted me conscious. I left my room and
reluctantly joined them. Sweet's loft, where his body lay in his bed,
was crowded with men in uniform struggling, grunting, swearing
as they tried to force his rigid form into a body bag.

A fat cop with a leather binder took notes. Turning, he motioned me over by waving his pen. "Know the suspect?" he asked, pointing with the same pen at all the commotion in the loft above us.

"Suspect?"

"Shit, sorry, I meant the deceased. It's been a long day."

"Yeah, I knew him," I said, and then turned my back to the cop to avoid having to answer any more questions.

"Know what he died of?"

The drugs I sold him? The oppressive atmosphere of today's society? The Agent Orange sprayed on him in Vietnam? The emotional toll of being a black man in America? Instead, I shook my head, and then stared at the floor.

"Found a marijuana pipe," he said. "Your friend smoke a lot of pot?"

Looking up, I noticed two paramedics coming down the ladder, half of Sweet's body slipping through their arms as they tried to get a grip. It didn't look like they were wrestling with a body, encased as it was in the black high-density woven polyethylene of the body bag. Instead it looked like they were just tugging on some fancy duffle bag with straps.

"You run into a lot of marijuana overdoses?" I asked the cop and then stepped forward, putting a hand out to steady the body as they lowered it to the floor. It felt hard against my hand, nothing like a human being.

"Somebody get a gurney over here," yelled one of the firemen. The body, prone at our feet, slowly curled back into the fetal position Sweet had died in.

"I'll never get used to that," said the cop as he looked away, shaking his head and closing his notebook.

•

It's late afternoon and I've just made the two-hour drive south from San Francisco to the San Joaquin Valley town of Santa Nella. The last time I was here I was trying to get to Sweet's funeral. There's a veterans' cemetery outside Santa Nella in the foothills of the Diablo Mountains. Sweet's family couldn't afford to bury him any other way than to let the Navy foot the bill—small payback for the time he spent in Vietnam. Because the car I owned at the time wouldn't have made it, I'd borrowed my mom's for the drive down. Late, as usual, I had pushed it to the limit all the way there. As I took the Santa Nella exit the car suddenly lost power. The motor was still running, but the transmission had chewed itself to shreds and wouldn't go any farther. Apparently my mother's mechanic hadn't refilled the fluids last time she'd had it serviced. Stranded just ten minutes away, the funeral already starting, I sat in the car wondering why I was always just this short of making it to wherever it was that I was going.

Sweet's sister drove back from the cemetery, found me stranded, and picked me up. By the time we got there, all I saw of the funeral was two cemetery workers standing around, shovels in hand as a bright yellow backhoe shoved the dirt over the grave. A raven flew overhead while the rest of Sweet's family wiped tears, hugged each other, and left in their cars. The wind started blowing, moving the tall dead grass by the perimeter fence as I stood there in that desolate place alone, out in the open, unprotected, thinking I'd seen some eerie spots before but nothing as foreboding as this.

I follow the signs for the San Joaquin Valley National Cemetery. Fifteen minutes later, I'm entering a low valley that looks vaguely familiar. More signs direct me to war memorials and areas reserved for veterans' groups. I ignore them and keep driving, but when I get to the center of the cemetery I realize I don't know where his grave is.

What looks like the main building turns out to be the information center, but the office is closed. A plaque by the door tells me there's 25,054 graves spread across 322 acres. To the left, built into a stone wall, is a computer that resembles an ATM. The instructions say to type in the name of the interred and the computer will dispense directions to the grave. A few seconds later, a printed map in hand, I'm in the car searching for the road to Section 3.

The graveyard is nothing like I remember. Although the last time I was here I was pretty strung out and stressed. Yet I don't recall it being as large and vast, and surrounded by all these empty round hills of bleached brown grass. The gravestones, granite markers laid flat into the ground in rows, hundreds, thousands of them, are barely visible unless you're standing directly above them looking down.

With a little difficulty, first driving into an unmarked cul-de-sac, then U-turning onto the wrong road and finally being stopped by a locked gate, I locate a small sign indicating Section 3 and get out of the car. I'm unsure of which way to go or where to begin and wander haphazardly, counting the rows, looking for the number of Sweet's grave. Leave it to the military to consecutively number everything.

Although there's not a living soul out here, there are the leftovers from past mourners. Vases with dried dead flowers and faded ribbons are everywhere. A large silver Mylar balloon, tied to the ground with "Happy Birthday" written along one side of it, sways in the breeze. *Not too happy a birthday*, I think as I almost step on Sweet's grave. I abruptly stop and stare down at the gravestone.

I'd been trying to remember when Sweet died. Last night I couldn't remember the date or even the year. Now, here it is in front of me, at my feet, etched in stone: "December 16 1994." I breathe in and something hits me hard in the stomach. Today's date is December 18, 2007. The medical examiner's report stated Sweet had been dead for two days before I'd found his body. Somehow, considering leap years, the earth's rotations, this is probably as close to the time, if not *the* time I found Sweet dead thirteen years ago.

I stare off across the field at all the other graves. I look back down at the ground. Inside I hurt. I feel lonely, small. I almost turn to leave, but instead I stand there. Then I begin to talk to Sweet, or at least to his grave. I tell him how well I'm doing. How things have changed and that I'm no longer hell-bent on killing myself—I'm not even sure he would recognize me anymore. I tell him how it hurt to see him dead. I tell him how much I miss him. I never really grieved over Sweet's death. Never grieved over anybody's death. I don't know how. Too caught up being somebody else that I thought I should be, instead of just caring and having feelings. Too caught up trying to be somebody else's idea of what a man should be.

I start to cry and even though it's awkward I don't try to stop. I wipe my eyes, the tightness in my chest slowly dissipates. I look down at the grave and say goodbye. Tell Sweet I love him.

On the way back to my car, I realize just how much of my past I've tried to forget. I've never acknowledged the dead. I've never put to rest the resentment I had toward them because I used the excuse they were dead. Only ignoring them hasn't worked. If it had, I wouldn't still be seeing them. Bad habits, wrong choices, hard living killed them—it's not my fault they're dead. I need to acknowledge they're gone and not coming back.

A couple of ravens stand by my car, large and ominous. As I open the door and get in they strut away, unafraid. It's been a long day and I've still got a ways to go before I'm home.

PART TWO

"No one can walk backward into the future."

— *Fortune Cookie*

THE PROCESS OF FORGIVENESS

SAN FRANCISCO, JANUARY 8, 2004

Dear Jenny

I ran into Alicia and she gave me your address. I really want to make amends for everything that happened. I am sorry for how fucked up it all got and for the way it all ended. I feel incredibly guilty for taking you down the road that I was on. You didn't deserve to be that messed up and strung out. I'm sorry I introduced you to the needle. Your life would've been much better if you had never met me. Not a day goes by that I don't feel the guilt and shame. I hope you can find it in your heart to forgive me. I totally understand if you can't. Here is my phone number and address—you do not have to contact me—I would've preferred to have done this in person, but I am not taking it for granted that you would even want to talk to me. I sincerely hope you are doing well, and that life has been good to you.

Patrick

Substance of Revelations

SAN FRANCISCO, OCTOBER 14, 2008

I sit scrunched down in the front seat of my car and watch a woman behind the wheel of a giant, gas-guzzling SUV casually pick her nose and then honk her horn. This is not where I want to be or what I want to be watching. But stuck in this rush-hour traffic, neither of us is going anywhere. In my rearview mirror, I see a line of cars stretching behind me for blocks. The situation in front is no different.

At Sixth and Mission I wait for the light and watch a couple of dudes in baggy-ass clothes hand off crack to a rail-thin woman with two kids in tow. In the crosswalk, a lumbering giant of a man slowly pushes a shopping cart full of crap across the street, never taking his eyes off the ground, like he's searching for something. When his cart hits the curb he stops, backs up, and rams the curb again. It's like he can't figure out what's in his way. He just stands there staring at the ground, pulling back his cart and repeatedly shoving it against the curb.

The light changes and I follow the other cars into the intersection and get stuck as traffic comes to a halt. Horns blaring, engines idling, drivers yelling and still no one moves. Up in the sky, glowing a brilliant off-white, is the biggest full moon I've seen in a long time. One of those harvest moons where it looks so close you can see the pockmarks, craters, and all that shit the astronauts left strewn across the surface.

It might be rush hour to the rest of the world, but down here south of Market Street it's business as usual as small groups of meandering dope fiends crowd the sidewalk, hanging out in front of the pawn shops and liquor stores. Most of them dressed in over-sized jeans and hooded sweatshirts, some carrying canes, a couple with carts, almost all of them holding brown paper bags with open cans of malt liquor inside. Sixth Street is still a fucked-up neighborhood, no matter how hard people with money try to gentrify it. When I heard they'd opened a new nightclub down here I couldn't believe it. Who'd want to be down here if they could help it?

The car in front of me moves a couple of feet and another car pulls out from its parking space, cutting me off. For a second I think about honking my horn, or somehow squeezing around, but it really doesn't matter. No one's going anywhere and one more car isn't going to slow anything more than it already is. Across the street, between the new trendy bar and the really bad burrito place, is a really good Vietnamese restaurant. Thinking maybe I should take the parking spot and get something to eat instead of sitting in traffic getting voodoo'd by the moon and bitching about how fucked up everything is, I pull to the curb and park as the other car's glowing brake lights slowly move away.

The night air is warm as I lock my car and slip through the stalled traffic and cross the street. When I get to the sidewalk I step around a woman sitting on a piece of cardboard, a dirty paper cup in her outstretched hand as she begs for money in a neighborhood where no one gives a shit. The stench of piss and rotting garbage is everywhere. The scent of burning crack comes and goes on the night air. Most of the block is unusually dark, as if the night has come too fast after such a warm day and nobody's bothered to turn the lights on. Shadows cloak doorways and back-alley sidewalks are littered with the dark lumps the sleeping homeless make.

Up the block on the corner a group of thugs stands in front of a brightly lit liquor store. A tall skinny dude in the middle of everybody is yelling and grabbing his crotch whenever a woman walks by and three youngsters dressed almost exactly the same laugh at every word he has to say. An older guy looking in rough shape walks up and hands one of the youngsters some crumpled dollar bills, another one hands him some dope. Then the tall skinny dude talks a bunch more shit, hassling the old guy, who doesn't even seem to be listening as he steps around the corner to smoke his crack.

I cross the alley toward the corner store and lock eyes with the tall skinny dude, then we both look away. When I notice the questioning look in the eyes of the youngster standing next to him, I shake my head no. When they realize I'm not a potential customer they go back to looking tough, their practiced expressions rigid on their faces. Nobody says anything to me and I keep moving.

Up the sidewalk a kid with a black hoodie covering most of his face is fumbling with something. Then I see a flash of polished steel in his hand as he starts moving toward me. Turning sideways, I step out of his way and put my back against the wall of the building. Then he's running past me. When he slams the knife into the tall skinny dude, all I hear is the wind being knocked out of his lungs. Like everything else has gone silent, but that's impossible. There's so much traffic in the street and people are everywhere, talking, jiving, making a fuss. There's even music from somewhere in one of the hotels lining the street.

Then someone yells. People start running. The tall skinny dude falls to the sidewalk. The kid in the hoodie disappears. Either he's run around the corner or down the alley, or maybe he's just faded back into the shadows—I'm not watching him. All I'm seeing is the tall skinny dude as he lies there motionless.

A group of people like myself, who haven't run, just stand there and stare, doing nothing. A woman in a doorway of a hotel pulls out her cell phone and calls 911, telling the dispatcher to hurry, someone's hurt. Then she hangs up and walks over to the tall skinny dude lying there on the sidewalk. Both his hands are holding his stomach, his eyes wide open staring up at the moon in the night sky.

"They comin', honey," she says. Then she walks into the liquor store.

I can't see any blood, but he must be bleeding. The kid in the hoodie shoved the knife into him a bunch of times. When he closes his eyes and lets out a long sigh, I feel something in the bottom of my stomach go weird. Without taking my eyes off him, I back down the sidewalk and then turn around and walk into the restaurant. Like always, the front door is open, even on the coldest of nights. The kitchen is up front, the counter in front of it. The place is crowded as usual, the air smoky, the smell of spicy food intense. None of the customers have any idea someone has just been stabbed less than twenty feet away from them.

The short man behind the counter who's been there for as long as I can remember asks me if I want a table or do I want to sit at the counter. But right now I'm not really sure what I want to do. I'm not even sure if I want to eat anymore and contemplate leaving. Instead I decide to get some food to go, and when I tell him, he yells my order to the cooks while I sit on one of the ratty stools by the door.

Outside in the street a siren echoes off the surrounding buildings, getting louder. A cop car drives past, its flashing lights a red and blue strobe effect outside the door. The old guy who'd bought the crack from the youngsters walks by staring at the sidewalk, shaking his head and muttering to himself.

I look down at my hands and wonder if I should have done something, anything, instead of just standing there. I mean what was I supposed to do? That woman had called the paramedics. And, yeah, the dude was hurt, but I ain't no fucking doctor. Still.

My cell phone rings and I flinch before answering. It's my little sister calling to wish me a happy birthday. We talk for a bit, but my head just isn't into conversation. When we come to a silence, I tell her I love her, promise I'll call her later, and then I hang up. This morning, somewhere between being woken by the Department of Public Works and their jackhammers outside my bedroom window, and later spilling coffee down my shirt at the café, I'd remembered it was my birthday. But after all the bullshit of running around all day, I'd put it out of my head. Fifty-two years old, I don't really do birthdays anymore.

The noise outside grows. People are running toward the flashing lights to see what's happening—the legacy of the streets played out one more time in gory detail. Leaning out the restaurant doorway, I see that the tall skinny dude is on a stretcher with some cops and paramedics standing around him. A crowd of people has gathered, pointing and talking and hanging out in front of the liquor store like it's some kind of social event. A woman in short-shorts and knee-high boots walks in my direction screaming at a man in front of her, yelling about how shitty his drugs are and why he gotta be such a motherfucker. The man is so loaded he can barely open his eyes. The woman lights a cigarette and calls him a punk. "Give me some pussy," he says and then nods back out as she walks away in disgust.

I haven't smoked in years and I ignore the urge to start again. Confused, I turn around and look at the short man behind the counter and he looks at me and we both just look at each other. This isn't my neighborhood anymore—it once was, but it hasn't been for a while. But what's more apparent is this isn't my scene anymore either. I'm a visitor in a place I used to feel at home.

"*Happy birthday, motherfucker,*" I say to myself and sit back down on the stool. Never my most favorite of days, this one about usual for how bad they can be, but they have been much worse. Eleven years ago I'd been out on the yard of some dreary correctional facility staring at the double chain-link fences and rolls of concertina wire and realized it was my birthday. It wasn't like I told anybody. There was nobody to tell. There I was, forty-one years old and locked up with a bunch of idiots trying to kill each other, and I knew my life was over. Incarceration is the biggest waste of time, the most depressingly violent environment. Futile and stupid, the useless monotony of every day being the same, aimlessly counting the days before you can get out.

Something about the way that kid had gone after the tall skinny dude reminded me of the way things jumped off in there. If you weren't aware you'd get wrapped up in it. If you didn't see it coming, it could just as easily be you.

The short man behind the counter yells that my order is ready. I hand him some money and he hands me a heavy plastic bag. I feel the weight and can't believe how much food he's given me. I look back at him and he smiles as I hand him another dollar for a tip.

I cross the street instead of walking back into all that craziness. Another cop car comes to halt, effectively blocking both lanes. The outbound traffic is worse than before. When I get to the other side I see an old neighbor of mine. He's standing there watching all the commotion, carrying the same day-glo yellow "Jesus Loves You" sign he's been carrying around for years. I don't know how he does it. It's not like he has a job or anything. But every day he's out here on the streets carrying that damn sign.

I nod to him as I pass, and as usual he looks right through me like I don't even exist. When I lived eight blocks from here, he was my immediate neighbor. His apartment was across the hall. For four years I saw him every day with that fucking sign—me going off to work as a drug and alcohol counselor, and him going off to walk the street.

Seeing him reminds me of just how much I hated living down here—about the worst part of the city to live in. But when I got out of rehab, I had nowhere to go. Wasn't like there were a bunch of places waiting with open arms for an ex-con/ex-dope fiend. After a couple of months laid up in a crack hotel on Folsom Street, I heard about a place over by the new ballpark. It was a government-subsidized clean-and-sober living, single-occupancy-only building, and I qualified as long as I held a job and stayed out of jail.

The rooms were three hundred square feet, a kitchenette and bathroom included. Not as small as a prison cell, but roughly as confining. I figure that's why they included free cable with the rent. With four hundred and fifty of these rooms in a seven-story building crammed on a corner lot underneath the on and off ramps to the Bay Bridge, there were a lot of people living in a small space, and a lot of crazy shit went on. Most of my neighbors were as bizarre, if not more so, than the sign guy. At least he was harmless, even if he didn't ever say hi.

The neighborhood was what they called "transitional." Which meant all the homeless junkies and crackheads still lived in the alleyways, shitting on the sidewalk and breaking into cars. New condo lofts for the yuppies went up as the old derelict buildings got torn down. Things were starting to change and nobody knew how to change with them. The yuppies hated the dope fiends, the crackheads hated the yuppies, and all of them hated anyone that lived in my building because we didn't belong in either category.

At this point I had less than two years clean and even the smallest events were challenging. I tried my best to live a quiet life and stay out of trouble. Restless and discontent and not really knowing what else to do, I got a job working nights, counseling parolees and addicts, but really I was just the overnight guy making sure nothing went wrong. In the morning I came home to my tiny room and cable TV and zoned out on Prozac the doctors had prescribed for my depression. But after a few years of medicated mediocrity I was left wondering if this was all there was to staying drug free. Ultimately I knew I had to do something different, but I had no idea how, or what different was.

Then one day walking home from downtown, there was this commotion and people were crowding the sidewalks and the cops were everywhere. I pushed my way through and lying there in a pool of blood was some poor fucker the cops had shot. And just like I did tonight, six years later, I stepped around the body as the blood drained into the gutter, and walked past it all. The cops, the body, all the blood and all the people staring and the whole time I'm thinking about what I'm going to do for dinner. Go out to eat or pick something up at the store?

I got home and sat down in my only chair, the lights off, the TV dark. There was something way too familiar about all this, and when I thought about it I remembered another time, when I'd just moved back to San Francisco from LA twenty years ago. I was living in the Mission and I'd come out one night to go to the store and there'd been these two drunks fighting. Neither of them spoke English, or at least they weren't saying anything in English when they were fighting. I stood and watched, and then one of them knocked the other one down and his body hit the concrete with a thud. Then the guy jumped on top of him and grabbed his head with his hands and started slamming the other drunk's head into the sidewalk. A pool of blood started forming. The man was obviously hurt. But the other guy kept beating his head into the sidewalk.

Finally some passing cops stopped and pulled their car to the curb. The one drunk still didn't stop beating on the other one, even as the cops got out of the car. When they pulled him off and put handcuffs on him there was blood everywhere and I walked into the store and bought some cigarettes, chocolate milk, and sugar wafer cookies—the three food groups I existed on in those days—and came back out as the ambulance pulled up. I lit a cigarette and stood under the streetlight and watched the cops make notations in their little black leather books. Then the old lady with her hair in curlers who lived in the apartment above the liquor store came over and stood next to me, an open beer in her hand.

"He kill 'im?" she asked.

"He ain't movin'." I offered her a cookie.

She took another sip of her beer. "I don't eat that shit."

The paramedics had covered the body with a dirty blue blanket. But the pool of blood kept growing and the cops cordoned off the sidewalk with yellow crime tape so nobody would step in it.

In the middle of the street was the police car with the drunk in the back seat covered in blood and handcuffed, staring straight ahead while the cops stood together in a small group talking and stealing glances at him like even they couldn't believe he'd beaten a man to death. I remember thinking how fucked that dude must have felt, but he was just sitting there, like he was waiting for something. I told the old lady goodnight, walked back across the street, and went home to shoot more dope.

Strange, I never really even thought about it again. I put it out of my head like it wasn't real. Like it was a movie or television. Or more like I was dreaming the whole thing. Except now it was way too familiar and eerily the same as what I'd just witnessed. Only these days I wasn't shooting heroin, I was munching Prozac.

The next morning I decided on two things: to get out of the neighborhood and to stop taking Prozac. It took me a month with the Prozac and two years to move.

Standing by my car with the bag of food, I look at the traffic and shake my head.

Across the street they're putting the tall skinny dude in the back of the ambulance, as one of the cop cars pulls a U-turn and then sits in traffic with its siren screaming. The giant man with the shopping cart moves slowly down the sidewalk behind me. He must have figured out how to get over the curb.

I close the door and I'm engulfed by the smell of ginger and garlic from the takeout food. I check the rearview mirror and see my reflection and realize a lot has changed in my life. I press down on the gas as I cross Market Street, and catch sight of the full moon between the buildings, shining down with all its tide-turning power and I feel the pull of insanity in the back of my brain.

At the next intersection a group of tough-looking teenage girls stands defiantly on the corner slinging crack to the locals. An old man walks out of a liquor store, a bottle in his hand. Two sleazy-looking dudes emerge from a porno shop, and a couple of trans-sexual hookers immediately accost them.

I mumble to myself about how some shit never changes as I drive up the hill and head home, the traffic thinning as I leave downtown.

The shit might not change, but the players do.

Karma on the Installment Plan

San Francisco, December 4, 2008

Superior Court of California
County of San Francisco

Summons for Jury Service

PATRICK SEAN O'NEIL

SUMMONS

You are summoned for JURY SERVICE on the week and at the place indicated below. Please read the entire summons carefully. If you are instructed to report, bring this summons with you. Failure to respond to this summons will subject you to a fine, a jail term, or both.

Your Jury Service Begins the Week of: Monday, December 01, 2008

LOCATION

Hall of Justice, Jury Assembly Room 307
850 Bryant Street, San Francisco, CA 94103

The line out front of 850 Bryant is ridiculously insane for 11 AM on a Thursday morning. Like the fall of Saigon in reverse, people are practically shoving each other out of the way to get inside. Defendants, witnesses, lawyers, visitors for inmates at the county jail, and lowly potential jurors such as myself being herded through metal detectors, while all our bags, backpacks ,and purses are being X-rayed as well.

There are only two metal detectors and two X-ray machines, and even though there's a half-dozen surly sheriff deputies standing guard, only two are manning the machines. Everyone is in a hurry, and there's a sense of panic mixed with hostile urgency. Most of us are running late or nervous about court appearances or jury duty. All the deputies, like wranglers running herd with cattle, are attuned to this, and when the crowd swells and attitudes flare, their response is to clamp down hard on any objectionable behavior. Unfortunately, after months of working this assignment, they're so fucking pissed off and tired they bark orders at everyone and treat us all like inmates at the county jail.

Every time I walk into the Hall of Justice I get weird. Then again, most of the times I've been here I haven't arrived through the front door. But the same deputies run the jails and the courtrooms and the threatening atmosphere they exude feels pretty much identical, even when I'm legally here at the invitation of a jury summons.

A woman behind me in line talks nonstop on her cell phone, bitching about having to wait. Every few seconds she stumbles into me and apologizes. She's so loaded she can barely stand. When she smiles and rolls her eyes, saliva drips out of her mouth. Pointing to the phone, she mimics someone talking with her fingers, apparently making fun of the person she's talking to. I'm a little taken aback by this show of intimacy and wonder how we became such close friends when all we've done is stand in line for the last fifteen minutes.

I received my summons in the mail a month ago. On Sunday night, the night before I was supposed to show up, I'd called the number on the summons, as per the instructions, and was told I wasn't needed Monday and to call back after 4:30 PM the following day. The way it works in San Francisco County, you only have to show up for one day. If you aren't picked for a jury that day, then you can go home. Your service commitment is over. But the twist is you've got an entire week where any of the five days can be your day of service, and you need to keep calling back until they either tell you to come in, or thank you and tell you you're not needed.

We haven't moved for a few minutes. At the front of the line there's a lawyer complaining to the deputies about them holding his client up, making him late for court. He's got his arm around some kid in saggy jeans and a baseball cap on backward. The kid looks like he huffs paint for a hobby and probably steals cars for a living. Not that I'm trying to judge him or anything. That's not my job.

The guy directly in front of me turns around and gestures with his thumb. "Fuckin' lawyers," he says.

I guess we're all starting to become one big happy family of subjugated citizens. Being under the thumb of authority makes us into community as we share the bond of being treated badly.

When I get to the metal detector I slip off my leather jacket, revealing the three metal bracelets on my left arm. One of the bracelets doesn't come off. Having put it on when I was twenty-one years old, my hands have grown. The other, a half-inch steel drive chain, is held on by a master link that takes pliers to undo.

The third one's thinner and silver and won't set the sensors off, but why should I take it off if I'm still wearing the other two?

The deputy shrugs and I place my jacket, belt, and newspaper into one of the trays and watch it move along a conveyor belt and disappear inside a steel box. I step through the detector, the alarm goes off, and I look at the deputy. She's not looking at me and I grab my stuff and step to the side and start to put my belt back on.

The loaded woman behind me is still talking on the phone as she steps through. The alarm sounds and the deputy yells at her to get off the phone and to go back and try it again. Instead of complying she starts arguing and then they both start yelling. The other deputies tense up and in unison push forward, an elbow shoves into me as they go by. I struggle to fasten my belt, and move to the side just as one of them asks the loaded woman if she wants to go to jail.

I grab my jacket and paper, then cross the lobby and find the elevators. Cops and lawyers everywhere: plainclothes, in uniform, and suits and ties merging in with the working stiffs, parole officers, and dope fiends in dirty street clothes either going to court or getting released from jail.

I wait for the elevator and a good-looking woman in high heels and a short black miniskirt walks up and I smile at her. She looks at me and smiles, and she's about to say something when we're interrupted.

"Hey, man. What are you doin' here?" says a disheveled short guy with missing teeth in his sneer. He's standing directly in front of me holding his pants up with one hand, and in the other, a manila envelope—the kind the sheriff deputies give you containing your personal property when they release you from jail.

"Hey," I say back, but I'm really not sure who he is. The woman in the miniskirt looks at me, then at him, then walks over to the elevator door at the end of the bank and stands with her back to us.

"Know this looks bad. I mean I'm just getting outta jail." He holds up the manila envelope as proof. "But I was doin' really good before this."

"That's good, man. That's good." I glance over at the woman's long, graceful legs.

"You remember me, don't you?"

"Well…"

"Still a counselor, ain't you?" He stares at me with an expression we used to call mad dogging. It's the look of the mentally disturbed as they are about to kill you.

"Stopped being a counselor over a year ago," I say, trying to remember if he was one of my clients.

"You ain't going to court?"

"No, man. I'm cool." The elevator arrives and I tell him good-bye. As the door closes I notice the woman in the miniskirt looking at me. I smile at her, but her expression is unreadable. And then she looks away again.

I glance at the control panel with its lit-up numbers and remember this elevator is only for the Municipal courtrooms on the second floor, Superior courtrooms on the third, and the county records room on the fourth. The whole other side of the building is the main police station and the top two floors are the jail, with their own elevators and stairs.

The door opens for the third floor and I step out and follow the signs to room 307—the jury assembly room. It's a big space full of chairs and tables and a couple of TV monitors on rolling metal stands. I show my juror badge that's printed on the summons to the guy at the front desk and take a seat in the middle of a bank of chairs set up in rows like a theatre. There's already fifty to sixty people spread around the room. Some of them have laptops, some are talking on cell phones. Most sit staring off into space or sleeping.

I open my newspaper and try to read, but I can't concentrate. It feels weird being here. Then my phone beeps. I've got a voicemail, but my phone didn't even ring.

"I'm in the hospital again. Call me. The number's 260-8000," says a female voice. There's uncertainty in her tone, a hesitation when she talks. I replay the message wondering who the fuck it is.

"In the hospital again?" I say out loud. The man sleeping in the chair next to me opens his eyes and looks around. I pick up my newspaper and try to read again. Then I realize it's Marisa who left the message. She's a girl from rehab, the one I wasn't supposed to go out with. We were both clients and at night we'd meet in the alley behind the detox and make out. She'd slip me her tongue and I'd shove my hand down her pants. But that was years ago and we haven't talked in months. Not since the last time her current boyfriend slapped her around and she called me crying. Worried he's finally beaten the shit out of her so bad she's in the hospital, I call the number.

"Psych emergency. Toni speaking."

"Excuse me?"

"Psych emergency, SF General—how may I help you?" Toni says.

"Ahhh, I'm calling for a Marisa Sanchez?"

"Please hold."

There's a click, and then some static. I press the phone against my ear and stare at the ceiling. The room gets quiet as the man I showed my summons to walks up to a podium and starts talking into a microphone.

"If I could have your attention please. I'd first like to thank you all for coming down today."

"Hello?" a small distant voice on my phone says.

"Hey."

"Who's this?" she says.

"You called me."

"Oh, hi."

"What's going on?" I say.

The man at the podium continues, "If any of you cannot communicate in English, or you're not a US citizen, we need you to come tell us now." He's got this sympathetic look on his face and I wonder if he's practiced it, or maybe that's why he got this job.

"I don't know. I was out drinking and ended up in the psych ward," Marisa says. "I got 5150'd again."

I really don't know how to respond. I mean what do you say when someone says something like that? For a few seconds we're both silent. There's static on her end. In the background someone is talking, I can hear Marisa breathing.

"I'm sorry to hear that, but I have to go, I'm in jury duty," I say. "Call you later, okay?"

"Okay, bye."

"While you wait for jury selection we're going to show you a video that explains what's expected of you," says the man, gesturing to the two TVs on either side of the room. "Now if you could all pay attention to the monitors we'll start, and please, those of you on computers and phones, turn them off and watch the video. Thank you."

Nobody moves. A few people don't even wake up. With a scratchy soundtrack of semi-evangelistic orchestra music the words "Juror Orientation" fill the screen, then a narrator briskly begins: "As Americans, we sometimes take for granted the laws that protect our freedoms. Trial by a jury of one's peers is among the fundamental democratic ideals of our nation."

I'd met Marisa when we were both in rehab. She was fresh out of the psych ward, 5150'd then, too. Maybe that was her reference to being in the hospital again. We'd hit it off almost immediately and against the rules of the program we had carried on an affair. Relationships are forbidden between clients, and when the staff got wise we had to sneak around and lie.

When I graduated, she was still there and we continued to see each other. Then the staff kicked her out for seeing me, even though I was no longer a client. She was stuck without anywhere to go, so I moved her into my room in the crack hotel I was living in.

At night I'd go to my job as a counselor in another rehab off in the woods thirty miles south of San Francisco. With just a year and a half clean it was hard keeping things together, and working nights didn't help.

One morning I came back to the hotel, Marisa was passed out in bed naked, and there were beer cans everywhere. When I woke her she held out a handful of Valiums, offering them to me. I stood there, almost reaching for the pills. If I took one I'd soon be shooting dope. I backed out into the hall and got another room. We were never together again after that, but we saw each other from time to time. Only I stayed clean and Marisa kept drinking.

•

Across the room on the TV monitor a scrawny-looking dude with curly hair and a mustache talks about his wonderful jury duty experience. "I believe that jury service is the essence of our American judicial system. It is the duty and responsibility of all citizens. If you are selected to serve, I hope you find it to be as rewarding as I did."

Then there's some sort of reenactment of a jury deliberating, although if this is meant to get us excited about the possibilities of jury service it's not working, and I start to lose what little interest I have. I fold the newspaper to look less conspicuous and turn to the horoscopes: LIBRA September 22–October 22, This is the day to tear up old scorecards and make amends. Even if you don't feel very forgiving, it's the gesture that counts.

The video ends and the man is back at the podium calling out names. Convinced I'm not getting called I keep reading, then I hear my name and I'm out the door with the rest of them to Department 27, second floor.

On June 30th, 1997, in Municipal Court Department 11, I was arraigned on two counts of armed robbery. I had just spent the weekend sick from heroin withdrawal in a jail cell on the sixth floor of the Hall of Justice and wasn't exactly responsive. I don't remember a whole hell of a lot other than thinking it was all rather strange and perhaps just an extended nightmare that hopefully I'd soon wake from.

I was standing in front of the judge in waist chains, shackles, and handcuffs, wearing jailhouse orange. There was a lawyer next to me, but I don't remember his name. My mouth tasted like shit and I was desperately in need of a cigarette. I heard the charges, and even after pleading not guilty, I still didn't think much of it.

I was in the middle of withdrawal, and all I wanted to do was get back to the holding cell.

The massive amount of dope I'd been shooting, plus the combined effects of the Valiums and Klonopins, clouded my memories. The robberies were vague images, as if I'd seen them on television. The first morning after I was arrested, I'd awoken in a twenty-man dormitory cell. Half the beds were empty. The rest of my cellmates were in the day room. Most were playing dominos, crashing them down loudly on the tabletop every time they made a move.

I was lying on the top bunk and when I got down I looked around at all the angry faces staring back at me, saw the bars, the chipped paint, the TV attached to the ceiling blaring rap videos.

In my back pocket was a yellow piece of paper, the carbon of my booking slip, two 211 charges, which I gathered were probably robbery charges. *At least I'm not fucking dead*, I thought, and went to take a piss.

The bathroom was a single metal toilet stuck on a wall out in the open. I started to pull down my pants and noticed a trustee in the shower stall smoking crack.

"What the fuck you lookin' at, white boy?" he said.

When I got back to my bunk I laid down and tried to remember what day it was, and how long it had been since I'd shot dope. I drifted in and out of sleep thanks to the residuals of the Valiums and Klonopins. But my dreams were horrible nightmares of trying to score dope and running from the cops.

It was night when I finally woke up. There were no windows. But I assumed it was night because all the lights in the cell were off, the corridor lights were on, and everyone was asleep and snoring loudly. I had stomach cramps and slipped off the bunk. Without warning, projectile vomit erupted from my mouth and sprayed the cell bars and shot out into the day room.

"Awww, shit," someone yelled.

"Mutha-fuckin white boy getting sick," yelled someone else.

"You betta clean that shit up mutha-fucka." I was pretty sure that last one was the trustee.

I stumbled across the day room to the toilet where I sat for hours wondering where all this shit coming out of me was from. I hadn't eaten in days. I'd barely drank any water.

I returned to my bunk exhausted, stepping around my puke. Out of the dark a person appeared and yanked on my shoulder.

"Clean that shit up, mutha-fucka."

The raging anger came from out of nowhere. I pulled his hand away, and slammed my fist into his throat. He started making a choking sound and began backing away. I lunged at him and punched him in the head, then hit him in the stomach. He fell to the ground and I was on him, kicking him, screaming. "Fuck off, man! Fuck off!"

Someone grabbed me from behind. "You done, man. Chill out," said a voice in my ear. I broke free from his grip and turned to face him. An older dude stood there, his hands open, palms out. "I got no fight with you," he said.

"Better sleep with one eye open, man," someone said in the darkness.

"Dude be dope sick. Leave that mutha-fucka alone. He crazy."

I went back to my bunk and fell asleep. When I woke it was morning. The old dude was tapping me on the shoulder. The deputies were serving breakfast: insulated trays of cold scrambled eggs, grits, plain white bread and brown liquid that was supposed to be coffee.

"You hungry man?"

I said no and he asked if he could have my tray. I told him yeah and got up and walked across the room to the barred entrance where the meals were being given out. When I passed the trustee, he was sitting alone at one of the tables staring at me with a black eye. He tried to mean mug me, but no one else was backing him up. I noticed my puke had been cleaned up.

"O'Neil, roll it up," yelled a deputy out in the hallway. I was being moved to another holding tank—the process of being reclassified due to the seriousness of my charges. With my six-digit bail, I could no longer hang with the common criminals.

There are at least ninety of us wannabe jurors in the courtroom, all crowded on folding wooden seats in the galley and even on the cushy armchairs in the jury box. A woman with a thick accent reads off names and the corresponding potential jurors have been instructed to yell "Here." In theory it shouldn't be that hard, but for some reason it is, and roll call takes forever.

My mother came to every one of my court appearances. I'd always see her there in the gallery with the rest of the families and friends of the accused. It seemed like I was in court every other week, either getting arraigned on more charges, or just holding it all over for another date.

At one of those arraignments the judge informed me I was looking at a possible three-strikes twenty-five-to-life case. The State of California had upped the ante and was now going to try me for three consecutive felonies in a row, a total bastardization of the three-strikes law.

With my hands cuffed, my legs and waist in restraints, I stood there dressed in orange and looked at the judge in disbelief. And then said something profoundly inadmissible like: "Are you fuckin' joking?"

The woman calling roll mispronounces my name, and it feels strange hearing it out loud in a courtroom. For a few seconds I feel like just getting up and leaving, not wanting to have anything to do with this monotonous due process of the law. When I somewhat reluctantly respond with a "Here," the roll continues, oblivious of whatever feelings or misgivings I may be experiencing.

Although this is not my first time back at the Hall of Justice, for some reason it is weighing a bit more heavily on me, and I am not sure why. In the last few years I've been to traffic court for running a red light and paid the fines downstairs in the County Clerk's office. I'd visited friends in County Jail, and when I was a drug and alcohol counselor, I watched clients of mine graduate drug court, an alternative sentencing program where they get sent to a rehab for treatment instead of jail. None of that really bothered me. I sort of went through the motions and did what I had to do and got out. But this time I'm not feeling part of it, and sit in the courtroom staring at the Great Seal of the State of California up on the wall behind the judge's desk.

Plea bargaining is a weird and mystifying process. The prosecutor states they want the maximum sentence, your lawyer—a public defender, in my case—states they want the least. Numbers, which are actually years, are thrown around, the lawyers speaking legalese like parents talking in code while the child is present. Both parties banter and chitchat, the judge looks on bored, probably wishing they'd do this outside of court. From my point of view it looked like everyone except me was on the same team, or at the very least was on good speaking terms and a little too chummy for my tastes.

Strikes and years appeared to be the main concerns. I was dead to rights for at least the one armed robbery. The others were speculation on the part of the prosecution, as there were similarities in method and what the witnesses saw.

Over the next couple of months I'd be offered various combinations: two strikes with ten years each; one strike with time served if I pulled state's witness and testified who was with me in all the other robberies; three strikes, one after the other, where I'd get a conviction, sent to prison, get sent back to court, get another and so on until I'd amassed three strikes and then be in prison for the remainder of my life.

Every time I appeared in court there were new charges and it seemed like the SF police department wanted to clear their books of every unsolved robbery. At one point the DA offered me twelve years and two strikes, and to tell you the truth I wasn't even really paying attention. My PD stepped away from the podium to confer. "Take the deal," he said. "It's the best you're ever going to get."

I looked at him and thought about twelve years. With two strikes, I'd do eighty percent, that's roughly nine and a half years in prison. "You take the fuckin' deal," I hissed.

With everyone finally present and accounted for, the bailiff calls the court to order and we all rise as the judge enters. Standing in the middle of the courtroom, he introduces himself and the attorneys. Then after he thanks us all he begins to explain the case. It's a robbery. A woman's purse was taken at gunpoint. The defendant claims innocence. There are no other witnesses and some obvious police misconduct, but the judge sort of sidesteps that issue. It's a case of mistaken identity and racial profiling.

I listen to the judge and think about how ironic this is and for some weird obsessive reason start to really want to get on the jury, to see what it is like to be on the other side. Although the idea of judging someone, or having the power over their freedom, isn't that appealing, the idea of seeing the wheels of justice in motion is.

When it became apparent that I wasn't going to be getting anything other than a lengthy prison sentence with the public defenders' office, my mother hired a lawyer. When I met him in the back corridor of the courthouse for the few minutes allowed, he flat out told me he didn't like me. He considered junkie scumbags such as myself to be worthless and the fact I'd been pulling robberies with a gun didn't help much either. But he said he liked my mother, felt she was a good woman and didn't want to see her get hurt. If I did what he said, he'd take the case, although he didn't think I had much of a chance. "You fucked up, man," he said. "The State of California really doesn't like rich people getting robbed."

He was cocky to the point of being smarmy and dressed in a nice suit with a perfect haircut. He talked a lot of shit and made me feel like the scum he said I was. But I knew I had no other choice. I asked him to please take my case—that I'd do whatever he told me to do.

"The first thing I do is keep postponing it," he said. "Get it so you're not the flavor of the month. You're no longer in the news, a little time for the dust to settle. Don't worry. Someone new will come along, someone worse then you. They always do. All you have to do is trust me, do what I say, and I'll get you the best deal I can. I'm that good."

The judge says that today he's going to address everyone that feels they have a hardship case for not being able to serve on the jury. Like if someone has too much going on at work, or they have a vacation planned with nonrefundable tickets or an ocean cruise to Tahiti. The rest of us should come back tomorrow at 10 AM. A dozen hands suddenly fly into the air. People start asking the judge a bunch of useless questions that only pertain to themselves. The judge says that these are the type of questions he will address and to please save them for later so that the rest of us can be excused for the remainder of the day. The questions continue. The judge looks annoyed. The entire jury room is restless. Everyone is trying to get out of having to serve.

The attorneys are calm, obviously used to this mayhem. When the questions finally subside, the majority of the room stays seated as the rest of us, the ones unable to come up with a ready excuse, leave the courtroom.

Outside, the day has turned cold. I pull my jacket on and walk toward Sixth Street. I didn't drive, because it costs too much to park. I can either walk to Third Street and catch a bus and be home in half an hour or walk down Sixth, past the spot where I saw a guy get stabbed last month, and catch a bus on Market Street, or wander around downtown for a bit. Then I remember Marisa, and call the psych ward.

The attendant on duty says she'll see if Marisa wants to talk on the phone and I stand on the street corner watching the commuter cars drive past on their way to the freeway.

"Hello?" She sounds tired, like she just woke up.

"Hey," I say.

"Oh," she says. "You called back."

"I told you I was going to."

"I know, but…" She trails off, leaving the unsaid accusation hanging there. We both know there have been plenty of times, like when she's been drinking, I said I'd call back and never did.

"Just want to know if there was anything I could do, if you needed anything." The psych ward staff isn't going to let me see her even if I try. And they sure won't let me bring her anything.

"No, I'm all right," she says. "They're going to release me at noon tomorrow. Maybe you could pick me up?"

"I got jury duty."

"That's right," she says and her voice sounds really distant. "Can I call you tomorrow, after I get out?"

"Of course." The walk sign changes and I start to cross. "I gotta go. Call me."

"All right, bye."

Another Day

in the Machine

Today the line is all the way out the door and down the sidewalk.
Fortunately I spot a few of the other jurors ahead of me, so I know
I won't be the only one late.

The deputy points to the bracelets on my arm. "You have to
take those off."

"They don't come off," I tell her.

"Then you can't enter the building."

"I'm on jury duty," I say. "You let me in yesterday."

She looks perplexed and scrunches up her brow. "Raise your
hands up as you walk through."

The second-floor hallway is crowded with jurors and defendants waiting for the courts to open. The noise level is deafening and reminiscent of county jail. Groups of young men stand
together yelling, and talk loudly about their cases. They all greet
each other as if they're at some social event and I guess for some
this is.

It all feels familiar in a really sad way.

County jail was insanely noisy. Dudes screaming at each other all
day and night. Different factions, different gangs, different neighborhoods: always fighting, always drama. Races cliquing up and

hanging together, calling parts of the jail their turf. Whites the minority, Blacks and Latinos the majority.

After I kicked dope, I started to feel better, then I had a grand mal seizure and started flopping around on the floor gasping for air like a dying fish while the deputies stood and stared—withdrawal from the Klonopins and Valiums. But the other kicking symptoms had subsided, and I wasn't shitting and puking, and I'd recently been able to hold down the lousy institutional food.

Now on the Seventh Floor of the jail and classified as a possible flight risk due to the severity of my charges, I was housed with parolees going back to prison and dudes looking at doing major time if convicted. Although the environment was still hostile, the unsaid rule was if you minded your own business, most of the time you wouldn't get bothered. Of course there were certain in-dividuals who couldn't follow rules, and fights broke out. Usually resulted in the deputies taking someone out on a stretcher. I was quickly adapting, getting numb to it all.

A runner for the dope man I used to buy from was put in my dormitory cell. After a couple of days he shit out the balloons full of dope that he had swallowed when he got busted. We made a deal for some commissary items. I bought some candy bars, cook-ies, and Cup-a-Soups and traded him for two balloons of his dope. Even though he'd washed off the balloons they still had the scent of shit to them, the dope did too. With no rig I had to dissolve the black tar heroin in a plastic spoon with water, then snort the liquid. I could taste shit as it dripped down my nasal passages. Five minutes later I was feeling the dope. I was in a nod and jail just wasn't that bad anymore.

The next morning I got called to court. Not wanting to be in possession of heroin while in transit—because you get searched before and after you go to court—I snorted the other balloon of dope in the holding cell.

My lawyer saw me nodding and scratching like a dope fiend almost instantly. "What the fuck do you think you're doing?" he said. "This is serious, they're talking three strikes. You get busted for possession in jail there's nothing I can do for you."

I couldn't look him in the eye. "Sorry," I mumbled.

"There's a drug treatment program in jail. I want you to ask the deputies to assign you to it. It'll look good to the judge, and eventually make a difference with your sentencing. But either way, whatever you do, stop getting fucking high!"

When I got busted, there'd been a drug charge, but it was soon dropped. The DA didn't want me trying to get leniency because I'd committed my crimes for dope. It was easier to get a conviction if I was seen as just a common thug terrorizing the financial sector of America.

I didn't want to go to the sheriff's drug treatment program. But then I didn't want to go to prison, either. Without a drug charge, I had a bit of a problem getting reclassified to be able to be housed in the Annex section of the county jail in San Bruno where the program was. Plus there was the problem of being strung out again, and I couldn't pass the required piss test. Fortunately, perhaps because it was unusual—not a lot of inmates ask to be sent to the program—I was reclassified and moved to the Annex. But not into the program, which was in D dorm. Instead I was sent next door to C dorm. The treatment program was full and I had to wait for an opening.

C dorm, a huge room filled with bunk beds, was sort of a purgatory waiting room for all kinds of misfits and mentally unstable prisoners that the county didn't know what to do with. It was a surprisingly easy time. No fights, no drugs, and I was able to lie around all day and do nothing, slowly kicking dope again, until it was time to be transferred out.

Twenty-two names for the first jury pool are called and I'm not one of them. Fewer than forty of us sit in the courtroom, assuming the other fifty must have had good excuses. When the prospective twenty-two jurors are seated, the court is called to order. The lawyers reintroduce themselves and this time we're introduced to the defendant. He's a young kid with dreads. He seems almost shy. He's definitely not one of those tough dudes out in the hall comparing prison sentences. Staring at him sitting in his chair at the defense table, I wonder if I can really do this. Be an unbiased juror. I'm already convinced he's not guilty. I'm thinking he doesn't look like anybody that'd hold an old lady up with a gun.

Then the judge instructs us all on how this is going to work. There's going to be questions asked of the twenty-two prospective jurors, each one of them will be polled. Afterward the lawyers will make their decisions while the jury is out in the corridor. Any juror contested by either side will be excused. Those of us remaining in the spectator gallery are the pool from which additional jurors will be pulled. So we need to be paying attention and have some patience with the proceedings in case we are called. If at any time there are any questions we should all feel free to ask.

The district attorney begins by asking each potential juror if they've ever had a bad experience with the police. A few of them raise their hands. It's mostly about cops being rude during traffic stops or not being considerate when they've been the victims of a crime. One guy says some cop accosted him and his friends when they were out drinking. The older woman sitting next to me rolls her eyes and says, "These people will say anything if they think it'll get them kicked off the jury."

"I know," I say, and then wonder how I'd answer that question. A woman in the back row of the jury box raises her hand and tells the court she hates cops and doesn't believe a word they say.

The defense lawyer says, "You really don't want to be here, do you?"

"No, not really," she answers.

Yesterday I was filled with lofty ideas about being a part of the judicial system. Today the patina of responsibility has somewhat dulled and the woman's statement doesn't really surprise me. But the old woman sitting next to me rolls her eyes again and whispers, "Oh no, she didn't say that."

I look over at her. She's totally cool, and totally right. I shouldn't be so quick to take the side of these jaded folks that surround us.

The questions keep coming. Do any of us have a problem with expert witnesses? If we were to hear testimony from the only witnesses to the crime, even if it was the victim, would we believe that person? Or would we need more proof? Do we know what burden of proof means?

Every few minutes the judge interrupts, reads a legal definition, or redefines a question presented to a juror. More hands go up, more excuses, more answers given in the hope of being disqualified. The process is numbing.

At quarter after five the judge abruptly stops the defense attorney from asking another question of juror eleven. "Ladies and gentlemen, be back here no later than 9:00 AM Monday morning," he says and steps from behind the bench to a rear door the bailiff is holding open for him.

The old woman next to me stands, straightens her dress, and says she'll see me Monday, unless I can come up with a good excuse not to come. We both laugh and as I walk out of the courtroom my phone vibrates with a text message: *u still in jury duty?*

It's Marisa. I can't think about her right now. I don't want to deal with anything. I'm tired. I'm not in the mood to be compassionate or understanding. I want to go home and sleep and check out from all this courtroom bullshit.

I walk up Sixth Street to Folsom and wait for the bus. Diagonally across the intersection is a neighborhood rec center with a bunch of kids hanging out front. A man with a shopping cart pushes past them and then starts crossing toward me. He's a really big dude with crazy long hair and full beard, lumbering behind an ancient shopping cart filled with large plastic bags and newspapers. On the front there's a hubcap from a Volkswagen attached like a hood ornament.

When the big dude gets to the curb he pushes the cart onto the sidewalk and starts rummaging around in the trashcan by the chain-link fence behind the bus stop. Intent on looking for the bus, I ignore him. Then I realize he's standing there staring at me and I turn to look at him.

"I remember you," he says and continues to stare.

I don't remember him. Probably another former client, all fucked up, homeless and insane, pushing a shopping cart, living in the streets. Silently I pray this isn't some guy I kicked out of rehab.

"I remember you from jails," he says. "Thought you was one a them three-strike mutha-fuckas? What happen? They let you out for snitchin' on sum body?"

"Excuse me," I say.

"You heard me, man."

I really don't recognize this guy. But how would he know about the three-strike charges unless he'd been there? In the criminal world, you don't go around calling somebody a snitch unless you're looking to get into some shit with that person, or you know it's true and you're trying to call them out. And part of me, that old me from back then, wants to get up in the motherfucker's face and tell him. But what's the point? These days I don't care. Really, what does it matter what this dude thinks of me?

"Don't remember you, man," I say. "And don't be calling me a fuckin' snitch."

"Same ol' fuckin' Pat," the big dude says, laughing. "You ain't changed a bit."

Then he crosses ten feet of sidewalk in two steps and he's towering over me, holding his hand out to shake, a big grin spread across his face. Cautiously I put my hand in his. The difference in size is ridiculous. It's like I'm shaking hands with a head of cabbage.

"You really don't remember me, do you?" he says.

And the truth is I don't. I'd figured him for another former client. But this guy is huge, not somebody easily missed.

"I was in a treatment program with you out at San Bruno jail," he says. "You was always talking shit. Reading that crazy writing of yours in group. I still think 'bout that story you wrote where you was gonna shoot a meter maid for givin' you a parking ticket."

This is too weird. I remember writing that story for one of the required educational classes they made us go to. I look up into the big dude's face and try to picture him ten years ago without all his hair and wild beard. When he smiles, I know who he is.

"Fuckin' Michael," I say.

"I knew you'd figure it out sooner or later."

And we both start laughing and then he hugs me and I almost die from the smell.

"Damn, dude," I say and push him away.

"Been a while."

The two years I was in county jail fighting my case Michael came in and got out about three times. He was one of those guys that when he got locked up he acted like it was at a health spa. Like he was taking a vacation from life. He'd get his hair cut. He'd take showers twice a day. He'd eat every bit of food served to him and ask anybody who wasn't eating if he could have theirs. Every morning after breakfast he'd be working out, doing push-ups and sit-ups, and at night he'd plant himself in front of the TV like he was at home in his own living room. If there was a domino game, he was in it. If there was a fight, he either helped break it up or joined in. When it was commissary day, he was always hanging around looking for a handout, and dudes gave it to him because everybody liked him.

Michael always requested to do his time in the treatment program dorm. All the counselors knew him and looked out for him. And the truth was he did really well in program. Talked a lot of good stuff, said he was going straight when he got released, and then a month later he'd be back and we'd all give him shit. Now seeing him out here in the street, all torn up, pushing a shopping cart and smelling like hell, it all made sense. But that was over ten years ago.

"What's up, dude?" I ask.

"You know. Weighing my options. Workin' a few angles. The usual," he says and laughs. "Shit, Pat, what the fuck you think is up? This is me, man. This is what I do. I wasn't one of you badass mutha-fuckas lookin' at three strikes. I don't do no big crimes. I just skim along on the surface, fuckin' up, going to jail. Keeps me alive, man."

•

When I got to D dorm I'd been off dope for two weeks. The second kick wasn't anything compared to the first. But I still wasn't ready for what was waiting for me. Sixty guys doing time in a completely separate part of the jail acting like they were in a drug treatment program. All day there'd be therapeutic process groups, educational classes, acupuncture, art therapy, and AA/NA meetings at night. We'd sit in groups for hours and talk about our feelings and fears and give each other feedback—which basically consisted of telling the person what a loser they were. At times it was all touchy-feely, other times it was brutal and hardcore dudes would be crying their eyes out.

But at night, when the counselors went home and we were left on our own, it turned back into jail and dudes would be looking at each other hard. The word snitch was often used, and when it was, the inevitable fight broke out.

Respect is one of those odd things in jail. Everybody wants it. But nobody is really giving it. Yet just say the word that someone is disrespecting you, and it's on. Time to get busy and fight.

Not used to being in either jail or a treatment program, I hung back, hovering around the edges, not getting involved. In the groups I listened to what people were talking about but didn't actually say anything. At the twelve-step meetings I bullshitted with the guys in the back of the room, there to get out of the dorm and do something besides watch TV or work out.

Everything I did was to look good to the judge. To show him I wasn't the hardcore three-strikes kind of guy the DA was making me out to be. Although I wasn't using, I knew that if they ever let me out I would be. It was just a matter of doing what my lawyer told me to do.

•

"So you never stay straight when you get out?" I ask Michael.

"Man, I try," he says. "But once I'm out there's no place but the streets. Tried a program. Lasted two weeks. Hooked up with some broad. Next thing I know we're holed up inna hotel smoking crack, doin' the wild thing."

A woman in a flowing black lace dress rides by on a bicycle—her legs a blur of black-and-white-striped tights, a huge radiant smile across her face. Michael and I stop talking and turn to look. Suddenly she starts singing, some sort of operatic aria, her voice trailing off as she rides away.

"Oooh," says Michael, sounding like a little kid as he reaches down, snatching a half-smoked cigarette off the sidewalk. "Got a light?"

"Don't smoke," I tell him. Then look up to see the bus coming through the intersection. "Later, Mike."

"Don't call me Mike," he says. "My name's Michael."

"Well, don't call me Pat either," I say. "Pat's what you do to a dog."

"Whatever," he says, and then he's back at the trashcan digging with both hands, the unlit cigarette butt hanging from his mouth.

After I'd been in the program for a couple of weeks I started hanging out with a group of dudes who were all facing possible three-strike convictions. Even though everyone admitted they were primarily there for the same reason that I was, the group was a little more serious about what we were doing. Most of the other dudes in the dorm were looking at short time, less than a year in county jail. Some were looking at a couple of years in prison, but that was hardly the same as doing twenty-five to life. Consequently, because of our status, the counselors paid more attention to us. Gave us more of a hard time. Made us do more in the groups, always reminding us what we were looking at if convicted.

While hanging out with these guys I started seriously looking at my life. I was forty years old and I didn't have shit. If I were to get out right then and there I'd have no place to go—nothing out there for me at all. My family would've helped. But they didn't want me living with them. I was a grown man, or at least the age considered to be, and shouldn't be asking for help anymore.

The bus pulls over at Pacific and Stockton and I get out. I'm tired and hungry. I need something for dinner. But I don't know what. The pungent aroma of fried fish hits my nostrils and I look in the window of the restaurant on the corner that's painted neon green. I ate here once with my father. The snow pea greens were good, but I think they were cooked in meat broth. Now that I'm a vegetarian, this is not a place that I frequent.

When you're locked up in county jail, food becomes important. Regular food is only served at mealtimes. But I was hungry all the time. My body was depleted from being strung out. It screamed for nourishment, especially since the State of California no longer allowed smoking in the county jails. I gorged on junk food and got fat. When I was arrested I weighed 125 pounds, and in a year and a half I gained another sixty. I became depressed. I thought a lot about suicide, only there wasn't any easy way to do it. My skin, already pale, became ghost white. My freckles faded, my hair started turning gray. My teeth became loose. My gums started bleeding. I felt like I was dying. Like my body was decaying. I'd look at myself in the polished steel mirrors above the sinks in the shower area and wonder who the fuck it was I was looking at.

At night, instead of hanging out in front of the TV with the rest of the dorm, I'd lie in my bunk and read whatever books I could find. Which wasn't easy at first. I hadn't read a book in years. But not being able to read scared me. I hadn't known I'd become so illiterate.

When I went to the educational classes I found I could barely read or write. I had trouble forming sentences. Words looked alien. I messed up the spelling. I didn't know the first thing about grammar or how it worked.

Every day I tried doing the newspaper crossword puzzle to build up my vocabulary. I read Stephen King and Robert Ludlum. Shit I'd never even think twice about reading before. But it really didn't matter. I just wanted to not feel so stupid. I didn't want to admit that I'd gotten so far out there it was like I'd never gone to school or gotten a Bachelor's degree when I was twenty and just beginning to dabble with heroin.

As I began to participate in the groups, the counselors started to notice me. When they found out I was looking at major time, they began singling me out—asking me shit like did I really want to spend the rest of my life locked up? Was getting high worth it? Was losing everything really a good option? At first I was angry at their attention. I resented their questions. I didn't want to have to think about any of those things. I didn't want to look at my actions or take responsibility for what I'd done. And even after all this time in jail, I still felt like this wasn't real—like I'd get out of this. Like I'd gotten out of every other bad place in my life.

When I went to my next court appearance, my lawyer called me out of the bullpen and said he had some bad news. "Looks like your friend Dolan is turning state's evidence against you," he said and handed me a manila envelope containing the transcripts and paperwork from the DA.

"You know you were offered the same deal," he said. "If you'd have told who else was doing the robberies with you, I'd have gotten your sentence reduced."

I remembered the look on Dolan's face when we were locked down that first night we were busted. "I can't do that."

"You ain't doing yourself any favors," he said. "With his testimony you're looking at doing some time."

On the bus ride back to jail I tried to read the transcripts. But the noise level on the bus was deafening and I couldn't concentrate. I was scared, depressed. It was all too real and I was going to get sentenced to twenty-five to life. When I got to the dorm I sought out Angel, another guy I'd gotten tight with who was also fighting a three-strikes case. I showed him the paperwork and asked him what he thought.

"You're fucked," he said. "This is how they do it now. The man offered you the deal, right? But you wanted to be a stand-up guy and didn't take it. So your homeboy did."

The next morning I went to group and told the counselors they were right. "I'm a loser," I said, "and I'm going spend the rest of my life locked up."

I unlock the front door of my apartment and step inside. The hallway is dark. All the lights are off and it's quiet. No one else is home. My roommates must be out somewhere. I'm so tired all I want to do is lie down for a bit.

I take off my jacket and boots and fall into bed. The room is cold. I shiver and pull the comforter around me.

CDC# P16921

I quietly slip into the courtroom and take my seat next to the old woman. "I thought perhaps you weren't coming," she says and smiles.

"I'm not a morning person." Rubbing the sleep out of my eyes, I notice the old woman is wearing a rather stylish suit. Her hair looks different. On her wrists and fingers she's loaded up with jewelry. "Looking pretty sharp," I tell her.

"Thank you," she says. "I wanted to look nice. They're gonna pick me today."

"They are?"

"Honey, this group is about to be excused," she says. "You heard them Friday. Jumping all over each other, trying their best to get the hell outta here."

As I glance across the courtroom I see that all the prospective jurors are seated in the jury box and the row of overflow chairs lined along the divider that separates the court from the spectator gallery. The DA is standing in the middle of the room looking at a sheet of paper in his hands. He shakes his head and then looks over at the public defender and then nods. Together they solemnly approach the bench and talk with the judge. The piece of paper is passed back and forth between them. The judge looks at the DA and shrugs.

"Juror seventeen," says the judge. "You're excused."

A juror I had never noticed rises from her seat, gathers her things and then hurries out of the courtroom. The remaining jurors look on as she leaves—a few of them rather envious.

"Good morning, ladies and gentlemen," the judge begins his long monologue about it being the defense's turn to poll the jury. I'm really not in the mood for hearing about the process of jury selection, although I listen when he says if they can't form a jury with who they've got, more of us will be called and the whole thing will begin again. Stifling a yawn, I tune him out and stare at my feet until it sounds like he's winding down. When he slowly reads from a list of names, excusing ten of the twenty-two jurors, I look around to see who's left, trying to figure out who they'll call next. Everyone looks tired and bored. A few people are reading newspapers, which is against the rules, but no one in authority is saying anything. I lean back against the uncomfortable wooden seat and try and stretch my legs in the cramped aisle.

Whenever I had to appear in court I was brought in shackled—a chain around my waist attached to the handcuffs on my wrists, making simple movement impossible—and dressed completely in jailhouse orange, my hair a mess, a few days' worth of beard on my face. For a while my attorney kept me from any real court appearances. Periodically I would show up and he'd waive my right to a speedy trial, citing he needed more time to prepare. Occasionally I'd get arraigned on more robbery charges. But usually I was only there to agree to hold it over for another date.

However, one time I was ushered into the courtroom in the usual cuffs and shackles and it was unusually crowded. As I looked around the spectator gallery I saw my mother and a few faces that were for some reason vaguely familiar, but not people that I knew. There was one row of women who all stared at me. A few of them were good-looking, and having been locked up for a year, I was intrigued, hoping they'd come to see me. Which was insane if you think about it. But that's how self-absorbed I was at the time.

As I stood at the podium next to my lawyer, I twisted my neck so I could look at the women and then noticed the man behind them was also familiar. In fact that whole side of the gallery was sort of familiar. Then I saw the cop who'd hit me in the face with the butt of her shotgun when they'd kicked in my door to arrest me. Next to her sat the detective from Robbery, and then the woman from a bank in the Mission who had refused to give me more money, even while my gun was pointed at her face.

My stomach started to tighten, my balls shrunk up into my body. I looked at my lawyer. He was talking to the judge. Then the judge asked if my lawyer had any last statements or objections before he began the preliminary hearing. I started sweating. My mouth went dry. I tried to get my lawyer's attention but he wasn't looking at me. For a second I thought maybe he'd made a deal with the court and they were going to sentence me to prison right then and there.

The woman from the Mission had hate in her eyes, and I saw myself as she possibly saw me—a violent thug who deserved prison. I looked at my mom, and she nodded. But she wasn't smiling and I knew I was fucked.

"Your honor," said my lawyer. "There are a few motions we have yet to declare. If it pleases the court I'd like to do so today."

I caught my breath and looked at my lawyer while he rattled off a bunch of stuff about illegal search of premises, illegal lineup for purpose of witness identification, denial of his client's rights, and an argument regarding the gun enhancement charges, as the police had never actually found the gun.

Sweat dripped down my face. I was soaked under the orange jailhouse clothes. I wiped my cheek against my shoulder and said yes when the judge asked me if I was in agreement with the motions. The judge said he'd take the motions under consideration and set a court date two months from then. I looked at the floor, avoiding everyone's eyes as the sheriff's deputies led me out of the courtroom.

The court clerk calls the name of a man sitting in front of me and he gets up and walks to one of the vacant juror seats. There are only two more seats to be filled and as I wait for the remaining names to be called I look over at the defendant and check the expression on his face as he watches the proceedings. He looks calm and somewhat confident. I wonder if I could have sat through my own trial, and then realize that if I had to I would have.

Another man's name is called and he gets up from the back of the room and walks slowly forward. I glance at the old woman. She's staring straight ahead—both her hands are in her lap with the fingers crossed.

"Patrick Sean O'Neil," calls out the court clerk.

I stand up, say excuse me, and slip past the old lady. There's a look of sadness in her eyes, but she smiles up at me. My juror chair is directly behind the defense table, two feet away from the defendant. At least I'm in familiar territory.

The only time I saw my lawyer was in court or in the corridor outside the bullpen holding cell right before court. Usually he'd tell me nothing was going to happen. "We're just holding things over," he would say. In court I was to agree with whatever he said. Mostly I just stood there while he waived time and then I'd go back to the bullpen and be stuck there for hours staring at the trash-strewn floor and smelling the stench of piss from the open toilet in the corner.

For months that was the routine. Back and forth. A long cold bus ride starting at 6 AM, appear in court for ten minutes, and then another ride back to jail at 3 PM. An endless procession of holding cells, inconsiderate transport deputies, angry inmates, strip searches, and a bag lunch of two plain white-bread-and-baloney sandwiches I never ate.

I came to dread the days I had to go to court. I always expected nothing to happen and usually was not surprised. One morning, stuck in the bullpen with a group of Nazi skinheads who were coming down off a meth run, I was called out into the corridor to speak with my lawyer.

"We have a deal," he said. "And I think it's the best I can do for you."

Surprised and not fully expecting to hear this, I said, "Okay."

"You get two years with two strikes. You do eighty percent of your time, and you get some off for the time you've already served. When you get out you're looking at three to four years on parole."

"No three strikes?" I said, and stared at my lawyer in disbelief. Over the past few months the DA had been offering a lot of different deals. When I didn't immediately go for them, he always went back to the threat of three strikes.

"No," he said. "The DA, the cops, hell, just about everybody thinks you can't do this. They're banking on you fucking up on parole and pulling another crime. Then they've got you for three strikes with no problem."

"It's nice someone has faith in me."

"Yeah, well, I'm not so sure you should take this deal. The DA might be right. You might be better off if I try and get you more time with only one strike."

"Why?" I asked.

"You have any idea the recidivism rate for drug addicts?" he said. "With only one strike, you catch another case and you'll do time, but you won't be looking at three strikes."

I wanted out. I didn't care what happened after that. I didn't know if I could stay clean, but I knew I deserved more than just being sent to prison for the rest of my life.

"I'll take the deal," I said.

"All right, if you're sure," he said. "But you might want to take some time. Think about it. Then let me know when you've decided. Once I tell them you're taking it, that's it. No changing your mind."

"I'll take the deal," I said over my shoulder as the deputy led me back to the bullpen.

Being inside the actual court feels even stranger than just watching from the spectator gallery. Somehow, crossing the divider has made it a little more real.

After cleaning his glasses, the judge clears his throat and asks if everybody is ready. Without waiting for a response he tells each of us new jurors to please state our full names, our occupations, and the neighborhood we live in. When the information has been recorded, the judge informs us that the DA will be asking the first round of questions, then the defense.

The DA stands, introduces himself, and then walks in front of us, greeting each of the new jurors. When our eyes meet there's a second of weirdness and we both look away. I felt my facial muscles tighten and I'm sure my stare had hardened. I wonder what that's about, then realize I haven't liked the man's demeanor from the very beginning. There's a pompous swagger to his gait and an obvious contempt for the jurors in his eyes and in the expression on his face. Which is stupid; I've been talking shit about all of them with the old woman. But I just don't want the DA to be able to have an attitude.

After asking each of us how we're doing, the DA starts in with his original question about whether or not anyone had ever had a bad experience with the police. The man sitting next to me raises his hand. The DA calls on him. The man describes a traffic stop. The cop in question was rude, the man felt abused. Another juror raises her hand and says her son is a cop—so she loves cops. The DA smiles.

When I think about his question I'm a little perplexed. Were my experiences with cops bad? They certainly weren't good times, but mostly it wasn't as if I was doing nothing and then out of the blue I was set upon by militant cops abusing their authority and trampling my rights. Cops in general aren't the most considerate of people when on duty. Yet when I was on duty, running the streets, robbing banks, and scoring dope, I wasn't the most considerate of junkies either.

Once, after being picked up for suspicion of auto theft, I'd cussed the cops out through the entire ride to the station, lying in the back seat handcuffed screaming my ass off. If I remember right I called them motherfuckers and pussies and told them they weren't shit. When we got to the station they dragged me inside and while we waited for the elevator I continued to scream my ass off. When the door opened they shoved me in and as the elevator started to rise one of them reached over and turned the emergency switch off and the elevator stopped and they both started to beat the shit out of me, each one taking turns punching me in the stomach and kicking me in the balls. In my memory the beating lasted forever, but I'm sure it was only a couple of minutes. Then they stopped punching me and turned the elevator back on.

Was that a bad experience? Hell yeah. But did I deserve it? Probably. Especially after the first few punches and I'm still yapping away telling them they're pussies and they hit like little bitches. But they never said anything the whole time. They just endured it and then kicked the shit out of me, and then turned the elevator back on and we rode the rest of the way up in silence. It was just part of the job.

The DA continues to rattle off more questions. Jurors respond, raising their hands, making excuses—both lawyers making note of the answers. Finally the judge interrupts and tells us we have a two-hour break. I get up and leave with the rest of the jurors who are rushing to get out the door.

"Guess I was sitting in the wrong seat," says the old woman when I run into her in the hallway.

"Believe me when I say, you have no idea how much I wish it were you instead of me."

"I know, honey," she says with a wave of her hand.

Jury duty pays fifteen dollars a day, plus two dollars and fifty cents for travel expenses, for a total of seventeen fifty. Minus a dollar fifty for the bus each way and I'm racking in a whopping fourteen fifty. With that knowledge in mind I decide to walk the four blocks to the quasi–health food store and hit their overpriced salad bar for lunch. Otherwise all that's close is McDonald's, a chain sandwich shop, or a taco truck across the street which, when

I stopped by last week to see if there was anything I could eat, had apparently never gotten the concept of vegetarianism.

Halfway to the health food store I remember to call Marisa and see how she's doing. Friday night we had texted back and forth, and then Saturday we talked on the phone and she seemed okay. Said she wanted to stop drinking. Only Marisa has said that about a million times, and usually she does stop for a bit. And then I don't hear from her. Then when I finally do she's fucked up and going insane. A continual cycle that only she can do something about. But I had promised her I'd call.

"Hey," I say to her voicemail. "I'm still in jury duty. They haven't kicked me off yet. Just checking to see how you're doing. Call me later if you want. Bye."

I have an hour left to kill before it's time to go back to court. I wander the halls looking into the various offices and police departments, and end up in the records room on the fourth floor. Then I remember when clients of mine didn't have identification;,I had to send them here to get their jailhouse ID: a copy of their booking sheet with their mug shot and date of birth that could legally be used for identification. Thinking that it would be really cool to see my mug shot I fill out the form and hand it to the woman at the counter.

"This'll only take a few minutes," she says as she enters my information.

It took almost a year in the treatment program before I started to really listen to the counselors. They'd all been where I was. Yet they had somehow made it out and gotten their lives together. One of the counselors kept asking me what was I going to do. Was I just going to do my time and then get out and keep shooting dope and pulling robberies until I was back here again? I didn't have an answer for him. But I knew he was right.

Then I heard that some of the other dudes were being allowed by the court to do their time in a program instead of locked up in jail. At first I had hopes that I could go into treatment as an alternative sentence. But the judge made it clear to my lawyer that I wasn't getting off that easy. The deal was the deal and if I wanted to make the treatment program a stipulation of parole, I was welcome to request that, but otherwise I was getting the strikes and doing the time, and that was it.

Still, it didn't matter. I came to the decision there was no future in using dope. So I started looking into residential drug treatment programs and found they'd come into the jail and interview me. Eventually one of the programs accepted me, and I made the resolution that when I did get released I was going there.

"Mr. O'Neil?" says the woman behind the records counter.

I get up from the plastic chair I'd been sitting in. "Yeah," I respond.

She hands me a color copy of my booking sheet.

I don't know what I thought I was going to see when I looked at my mug shot. Perhaps a tough-looking dope fiend doing the hard stare at the camera. But that's not what I'm looking at. What I'm looking at isn't very pretty. Staring out from the paper is an unfamiliar dejected-looking dude with an emaciated, pasty face. His eyebrows appear to be missing, and he's in need of a shave. But the worst is the look in the eyes.

"Thanks," I say and carefully fold the paper in half and stuff it into my jacket pocket. I really don't want to look at it anymore.

•

I'm still thinking about my mug shot when I walk into the courtroom. It feels like everyone is staring at me. I'm self-conscious and
wonder if it's obvious. I take my seat in the juror chair and stare
at the floor avoiding eye contact. I glance up when the bailiff an-
nounces, "All rise" and notice the DA is looking at me too. I'm
suddenly paranoid he's run my name and found out I'm an ex-
felon and is wondering why I haven't said anything. I close my
eyes and concentrate on my breathing, tell myself that it's not all
about me.

"You okay?" says the old woman as she leans over the divider
and touches my shoulder.

"Bad lunch."

"You didn't eat at that taco truck?" she says, her one eyebrow
rising in a question.

"No." I laugh, suddenly feeling better. "Thanks for checking
though."

The deal, like most plea bargains, took forever. But thankfully I
didn't have to appear in court anymore. My new dilemma was
telling the rest of the three-strikes crew I was getting out soon. Not
that I didn't want to tell them—I was fucking stoked not to be
looking at twenty-five to life any longer—but it's hard to tell that
to someone who is. When I finally told Angel, he was cool about
it and even hugged me. "But keep it to yourself, dog," he told
me. "Don't know which one-a-these mutha-fuckas might catch a
feeling and do something stupid. Act the fool and get you in a bad
way where ya gotta get busy and fight. Don't want that kinda shit
on your jacket right now. Know what I'm sayin'?"

With the rise in drug arrests and the new public awareness of

rehabilitation instead of incarceration, the in-jail treatment program was growing too big for D dorm. The sheriff's department
made plans to move the whole thing to the new jail on Seventh
Street, right behind 850 Bryant. The program took a few of us
along as the inmate/clients who were setting an example, doing
the right thing.

Now, instead of being housed in a cavernous dorm out on the
edge of suburbia, we were in the middle of the city, in a state-of-
the-art two-tiered round cellblock the deputies called "B pod." The
floors were carpeted and the bathrooms were clean. The cells had
glass doors, and everything was new. The only drawback was there
was no exercise yard and we never went outside.

At night, locked in a two-man cell on the upper tier, I could
look out the three-inch-wide slit of a window and see the city, its
lights shimmering as cars sped by in a blur of taillights on the 101.
I knew I wasn't going to be in here much longer, and seeing the
traffic and people walking on the streets below, I just wanted to get
the fuck out and never come back.

"Juror number twenty-two, Mr. O'Neil," says the DA, "if only one
witness testifies, would you be able to accept their testimony, or
would you need more information to come to a conclusion?"

I had heard the DA ask this question earlier and I thought it
was weird. Obviously there are some discrepancies with this case
involving only the victim's identification of the defendant. Staring up at the DA, I uncross my legs and take a moment before
I answer. "I think that like any decision I make, I would to need
to hear the testimony and see the person testifying before I could
fully answer that question. But, of course, I would accept their
testimony and I would use it like any other information to come

to a conclusion when all the facts have been presented."

The DA looks at me and makes a note in the folder he's carrying, then turns to another juror and asks her the same question. When I turn my head I catch the defendant staring at me. There's a look of sorrow in his eyes and he can't be much older than twenty-one or twenty-two. I can't understand why he would decide to take this case to trial. Nobody goes to trial anymore unless they're innocent or it's a three-strikes case. You plea bargain this shit unless your life is on the line—which leads me to think that maybe he does have past felonies and this is his third strike.

It was a much different atmosphere when I went to court for the last time. There were no other prisoners waiting to see the judge. It was just my case being heard and everyone involved had previously agreed on the outcome. The courtroom was quiet. The only people in the gallery were my mom and stepfather, my little sister and her husband, and Alicia. I wasn't handcuffed or shackled. The DA wasn't being his usual aggressive self. My lawyer was being very congenial, joking with the court clerk and smiling at everyone, including me.

I had never met the judge before. This was Superior Court. All my other appearances had been in Municipal courtrooms. But the deal had been struck and all I had to do was say yes and it was over and I'd be a convicted felon—California Department of Corrections prisoner number P16921.

"Good afternoon, Mr. O'Neil," said the judge. "I gather that we're all in agreement here and that this is just a formality, with you going on record and accepting the plea bargain your lawyer, the DA, and myself have worked out."

"Ah, yes, your honor," I responded and surveyed my surrounds.

None of it felt real. It was like I was in a dream. I had never considered what it was going to feel like to be convicted and to have my future decided by others. I knew this was going to happen. I wasn't stupid, or at least not naïve about the proceedings. I had just never visualized any of this actually occurring and it felt strange. As if I were watching it all happen to someone else.

The judge then read off the details of the deal: the two charges of armed robbery, the amount of time to be served, the amount of time I'd already served, and the conditions of parole.

"Mr. O'Neil, do you understand and agree to the convictions and conditions I have outlined and discussed?"

"Yes, your honor, I do."

"Mr. O'Neil, you do understand that by accepting two strike convictions at one time, that if you ever are charged with another crime you will be facing three strikes. You do understand and accept this, do you not, Mr. O'Neil?"

"Yes, your honor," I responded.

"I'd like the record to show that Mr. O'Neil understands and accepts the convictions and conditions," the judge said to the court reporter. Then he asked me two more times, wording the question a little different each time, if I understood that I was accepting two strike convictions. And both times I answered that I did. Obviously this was what my lawyer had previously warned me of. And now having accepted the convictions and going on record three times saying I understood, my next arrest would lead to a three-strikes conviction. I was putting my fate in the hands of the State of California's notoriously screwed-up judicial system.

The DA tells the judge he has no further questions for the jury. The judge then instructs the defense to begin. A juror interrupts and asks if the case involves mistaken identity, then who is being mistakenly identified. The defense smiles and points to the defendant. The defendant shrugs and looks at the floor.

None of the other jurors have said they have a criminal record. They all seem pretty honest. In fact, most of them have been overly generous with disclosing who they are. I start to feel that I'm not really being totally open by omitting the truth. I look at the judge and think of the mug shot I've got folded in my pocket. I wipe my hands on my pants and go back to concentrating on my breathing to try and calm my anxiety.

Finally, the defense signals the judge that he is done and then turns to face us all and asks if there is anything any of us wants to say before we are sent out of the courtroom. I stare at the floor and feel the muscles in my chest tighten and then raise my hand. "Juror twenty-two. You have something to tell the court?" says the defendant's lawyer.

"In 1998 I accepted a plea bargain for two counts of armed robbery," I say and think I hear a few audible gasps in the audience behind me. "Of course, that was ten years ago. I completed my parole, and since then I haven't had any personal dealings with the law. However, in a professional capacity for my former employment as a drug and alcohol counselor, I've had numerous encounters with the judicial system: testifying in court and writing letters for clients in an effort to obtain alternative sentencing to residential rehabs instead of jails, and attending my clients' graduations from drug court. I used to also deal with their parole and probation officers on a regular basis. And although I feel that none of that has any bearing on my ability to be a confident and unbiased juror, I still feel inclined to be honest about myself and hold no secrets from the court."

"Well, I'm sure the prosecution is happy you did," says the defense lawyer. The DA sits turned around in his seat staring at me with an expression I can only describe as relief.

"Mr. O'Neil," the judge addresses me, "I'm curious. It's obvious to me that you've come a long way since 1998, and I commend you for not only your honesty, but for the evident internal psychological work you've done on yourself. However, what I'm curious to know is if you think that because of your experiences do you feel you'd be pro prosecution, wanting others to experience hardships such as you have in order for them to see the need to better themselves? Or, ah…do you think you're more inclined toward leniency and rehabilitation?"

"I'd have to say the latter, your honor. Although I would also like to add that it is entirely a case-by-case decision. And I would hope that any juror would weigh the facts before making a decision on someone's life. But I have no illusions as to our roles in society. The oppressive police presence just getting into the Hall of Justice is only one small example of the lines that are drawn between the judicial system and the public. And although it is a flawed system, it is the only one we've got. And that's why I am here, to do my part."

The courtroom is silent. No one moves or says a word and I suddenly realize my anxiety is gone. Even though I can feel people looking at me, my confidence is back and I don't feel so self-conscious anymore.

Clearing his throat again, the judge breaks the silence and tells us all we're to return to the corridor for another twenty-minute break. Everyone rises and crowds together as we all file out into the corridor. Even though we are right next to each other in line, the old woman doesn't say anything to me and instead of sitting on one of the benches where we usually sit together she walks off toward the bathrooms.

Leaning against the wall, I check my phone, relieved to see that no one has called. A few of the other jurors are looking at me, but when our eyes meet they quickly look away. Then a woman who has been one of the jurors from the very beginning comes over and introduces herself.

"Hi, I'm Fran," she says. "Like what you said in there."

"Thanks, Fran," I say. "I'm Patrick, glad to meet you."

"You a friend of Bill W?"

"Who?" I say and then realize she's referring to Bill Wilson, the original founder of Alcoholics Anonymous. "Ah, sort of. Although I'm more familiar with another fellowship."

"Thought so," she says. "I have twenty years sober."

"That's great, Fran. Congratulations."

"Oh, I don't even think about it anymore," she says. "Just wanted you to know that you're not the only one in there."

"Thanks," I say. The old woman walks past and then takes a seat on one of the benches farther down the hall.

Ten minutes later we're all back in court. The lawyers have made their decisions and the judge reads off a list of those excused. And although I am not one of those excused, I am also not one of those that's picked. It's like I've just been left out, and now with the jury filled there's no need to even deal with me. In the confusion of people leaving and others taking their assigned seats I quietly get up and leave the courtroom and go upstairs to room 307 and inform the woman working behind the counter that I'm done with my jury service and to please make a note of it.

With my civic duty finally over I throw my crumpled jury summons in the trash and walk down the hall to the stairs. The sign on the door says "Authorized Personnel Only." Three flights later I walk across the lobby and out the front door of the Hall of Justice into the cold graying afternoon and put on my sunglasses. It feels good to know that I'm not coming back any time soon.

Author's Note

Memory isn't always clear. It can be vague, misleading, hard to penetrate, and at times so murky and opaque one can barely see into, let alone through, it. Add in copious amounts of narcotics, stress, insanity, depression, fear, anger, resentment, desire, and the passing of years and you have what I have—memories. Whether these memories actually happened exactly as I recall is possibly subject to discussion. Yet it isn't as if I'm lying, or just sort of making shit up as I go along. Given a polygraph test I'd pass. In a court of law I'd swear on a Bible. And from me to you—this is my truth. Although experts do contend that eyewitness memory is notoriously unreliable. And I understand this. However there are memories that do not go away: a horrific incident, the death of a loved one, a wondrous occasion, are all events we say we'll never forget—and we don't. So take it from me, the adrenaline rush of an armed robbery, your best friend being murdered, a narcaine injection bringing you back from the dead of an OD for the seventh time, the click of handcuffs, or the slam of a cell door—these are moments I'll never forget. No matter how hard I try. And these are the memories that I have given you in this book. Some names were changed, as well as times, dates, places, and in a few places the actual chronological order of events. This was done for the obvious reasons: protecting identities and self-preservation.

Acknowledgments

A lot of people helped me along the way in life and with writing this book and I'd like to acknowledge them. Wayne O'Neil, for being who you are and reading all the bad first drafts. Donna Francesconi, for your support and love. Scott, Liz, Dylan, Maya, and Jennifer: you are the women in my life that make it worth living. Rob Roberge, for all the late-night phone calls, voluminous texts, words of wisdom, and being a true friend. Eric Vieljeux, Patrice Carrer, Bernadette Murphy, Emily Rapp, Rachael Toor, David Ulin, Bernard Cooper, Bad Bill Garnett, Antonia Crane, Consuelo Flores, Don Lattin, Anne Canright, Mariel Howsepian Rodriquez, and Barbara Lewis—for your edits, suggestions, critiques, support, and even some harsh words of reality. Abie Stillman, because, well, you know why. Anna-Lisa S. VanderValk for being there. Gina for forgiving me. Jerry Stahl—thanks for France. And last, but definitely not least, Guy Intoci for having faith in me, the fortitude to keep pushing my book, and the vision to make it better.

Printed in the USA
CPSIA information can be obtained
at www.ICGtesting.com
JSHW022221140824
68134JS00018B/1191